W9-CLA-950

GLOUCESTER MASSACHUSETTS

# PAPER**HOUSE**

## handmade paper crafts for your home

MARY ANN HALL

ROCKPORT PUBLISHERS

WITHDRAWN
No longer the property of the
Boston Public Library.
Sale of this material benefits the Library

Copyright © 2001 by Rockport Publishers, Inc.
All rights reserved. No part of this book may be
reproduced in any form without written permission
of the copyright owners. All images in this book
have been reproduced with the knowledge and
prior consent of the artists concerned and no
responsibility is accepted by producer, publisher, or
printer for any infringement of copyright or otherwise, arising from the contents of this publication.
Every effort has been made to ensure that credits
accurately comply with information supplied.

First published in the United States of America by
Rockport Publishers, Inc.
33 Commercial Street
Gloucester, Massachusetts 01930-5089
Telephone: (978) 282-9590
Facsimile: (978) 283-2742
www.rockpub.com

ISBN: 1-56496-782-4
10 9 8 7 6 5 4 3 2 1
Design: Leeann Leftwich
Front cover images: Mary Ann Hall (top left); Connie
Sheerin (top right); Mary Ann Hall (bottom left);
Livia McRee (bottom right)
Back cover images: Mary Ann Hall (all images)
Photography on pages 8, 11-13, 26, 37, 38, 39, 65-67,
108 by Graphics Atlanta, Malvern, Pennsylvania

Printed in China.

TT870
.H23
2001

4   INTRODUCTION: PAPER BASICS

8   PAPER LIVING ROOM

26   PAPER WINDOWS

44   PAPER KITCHEN

62   PAPER BEDROOM

84   PAPER BATH

98   PAPER CRAFTS GALLERY

121   CONTRIBUTING ARTISTS

122   RESOURCES

124   PATTERNS

127   ACKNOWLEDGMENTS

128   ABOUT THE AUTHOR

"BLESSED ARE THEY WHO SEE BEAUTIFUL
THINGS IN HUMBLE PLACES WHERE
OTHER PEOPLE SEE NOTHING."
CAMILLE PISSARRO

**IT'S SO EASY** to take paper for granted; our lives are full of it. But it's worth taking a closer look at this wonderful and versatile material. This book shows how paper can be used almost anywhere—on walls, floors, windows, and furniture. Paper can be transformed into a bowl, a runner, or a serving vessel. There are endless possibilities and the techniques are simple—paper is forgiving, easy, and fun to work with. Also, relatively speaking, paper is affordable. The beauty of using paper in the home is that it's a material that can allow you to change or update your furnishings regularly without huge expense.

Wonderful papers of all sorts are widely available. Although a majority of the projects in this book use handmade papers, others use mold-made papers, tissue, magazine scraps, recycled papers, and card stock. Some of the projects also use materials that, technically speaking, are not really paper at all, such as vellum. If your appreciation of handmade papers grows as you experiment with various projects presented here, I encourage you to explore the process of making paper yourself.

**What is Paper?** True paper is a compact web of raw materials that have been macerated (beaten) until each of the fibers is a separate element. The underlying techniques for making paper have remained fundamentally unchanged for over two thousand years. The fibers are mixed together with water and then lifted with a screen that catches the fibers as the water drains through. The fibers join together when they are pressed and dried to form a sheet of paper.

## TYPES OF PAPER

**Handmade paper** is paper that is made in individual sheets by hand in a traditional manner, that is, by using a mold to catch the fibers. The fibers are drained on a bed of felt and left to dry in stacks known as *posts*. Because handmade paper is shaken evenly on the mold, it doesn't have a grain. The resulting untrimmed and irregular edges of a handmade sheet of paper are called *deckle edges*.

**Mold-made paper** is made on a cylinder mold machine and closely resembles handmade paper because it has long fibers and is strong. The initial pulp preparation is similar to that of handmade paper, but a machine is used in the formation of the sheet. Essentially, a cylinder covered with a metal screen revolves through a vat of pulp, forming a long continuous sheet called a *web*. The web is surrounded by felts and is then passed through pressing and heating areas. Eventually, the web is divided into sheets by hand, producing two torn edges and leaving two true deckle edges. Mold-made paper is a good substitute for handmade papers if economy is an issue.

**Machine-made papers** have been produced for about two hundred years. Because they are geared for consumption and disposal, they use inexpensive materials and have chemical additives. The resulting products are often unable to withstand the ravages of time. However, since 1970, some improvements to higher-range artists' papers have been made, creating papers with more permanence. Therefore, you can find high-quality, acid-free, machine-made papers that are perfectly suitable for certain projects. The advantages of machine-made papers lie in their uniformity, affordability, and availability.

## WHAT IS ACID-FREE?

The majority of artists' papers today are labeled as acid-free. This means the paper will age well without yellowing or becoming brittle. Acid-free paper is important for books or artwork that are made to last, but is not as important for the types of projects presented here: if you create paper shades for your windows or a paper tablecloth for your kitchen, it's unlikely that you will keep them for hundreds of years.

## CHOOSING PAPERS

There are many factors to consider when choosing papers for a project:

### Translucency and Opacity

This is the degree to which light can be transmitted through a paper. To test the translucency or opacity of a sheet, tilt it at various angles against a light source. For projects like candle shades, lamps, and window treatments, choose translucent paper that allows light to pass through. If you are going to create a surface design or print with your papers, you may want to choose a more opaque paper that will not reveal the pattern on the reverse side.

### Weight

Gsm, or grams per square meter, indicates paper weight. Occasionally, the weight is given in pounds per ream; a ream is five hundred sheets. Lightweight papers include tissue, lace papers, and many Japanese papers. Papers similar in weight to those you use daily for writing are generally between 80 gsm and 120 gsm or 60 pound to 80 pound and are considered light- to medium-weight papers. Medium- to heavy-weight papers range from 150 gsm to 220 gsm. Card stock is around 225 gsm.

### Strength

Japanese handmade papers, often referred to by the generic designation "washi," are made of tough and durable bast fibers, such as mulberry. They can be employed for a far wider range of uses than rag or wood-pulp paper.

### Grain

The grain of a paper refers to the alignment of fibers within the sheet. Most handmade papers have little or no grain because the fibers are randomly distributed across the mold when they are made. Papers with no grain will be equally strong in both directions and will remain stable under variable conditions. Papers made on molds that run along a moving belt will have a grain that runs in the direction that the belt is moving.

Paper tears more easily with the grain than against it. However, if you wish to have a rough tear, you may wish to tear the paper in the direction opposite the grain.

It is easier to fold a paper along the grain than across it, but folding endurance is stronger across the grain because paper is less likely to tear across the grain. Folding with the grain will produce a clean edge that leaves the paper nice and smooth. In humid conditions, paper will absorb more moisture and expand more across the grain than along it. In dry conditions, it will contract more across the grain.

## BASIC TECHNIQUES

### Tearing

Sometimes it's preferable to use papers with a torn edge rather that a cut edge for a project. A torn edge will be softer and look more natural. For a clean, even edge, tear with the grain. For a rough, ragged edge, tear across the grain. To tear a straight line, lay a metal ruler over the line you want to tear. Place your weight on the ruler with one hand. Use the fingers of your other hand to pull the paper up and across the edge of the ruler. To create the look of a natural deckle edge or to help tear a thick paper, wet the line to be torn using a paintbrush, then use the ruler method described above to pull the wet fibers apart.

### Cutting

Always use a sharp blade and work on a cutting mat. Cutting mats are useful to help align and measure your pieces as well as to protect your work surface. Hold the paper firmly down with a straightedge and keep your fingers away from the cutting edge to avoid accidents. Cut along the straightedge with the blade. Don't remove the straightedge before checking that the paper is completely cut through. You may need to run the blade through twice.

### Folding

Work precisely to obtain clean, crisp folds and use a bone folder. Bone folders are simple tools, pointed on one side and blunt on the other, used to create clean folds. Remember, is it easier to fold with the grain. Mark out spaces at the top and bottom and, if necessary, in between where each fold should go. For each fold, draw a bone folder along the straightedge, pressing lightly. This is called *scoring*. Then, fold along this indented line using the edge of your ruler as a guide. Complete each fold by smoothing it firmly with the bone folder.

### Gluing

PVA (polyvinyl acetate) is an excellent all-purpose, acid-free adhesive to use for most paper projects. Also known as white glue, it is a quick-drying, plastic-based adhesive that keeps paper flat and dries clear. When diluted, it can also be used for sealing porous surfaces. Apply glue with a brush. Use a stippling action or brush the glue from the center out to ensure all areas are covered.

Decoupage medium is a water-based glue, sealer, and finish that can be used for applying paper to all surfaces. It can be applied with a brush or a sponge and provides a strong, permanent surface once dry. It is available in a variety of finishes from matte to satin to gloss.

Acrylic matte medium is opaque when wet and translucent when dry. It can be used for collage and works well in adhering paper to glass. It produces a matte, non-reflective finish.

### Finishes

For paper projects that will receive wear and tear, such as furniture or other functional pieces, you should coat your paper with a protective finish. This finish will protect the paper and waterproof the surface. Apply finish coats with a sponge or bristle brush, taking care to follow specific manufacturer's instructions. Usually, multiple coats are recommended.

Acrylic varnish is a water-based finish that can be used to coat and protect any paper project. It is available in matte and satin varieties. Because it dries quickly, before dust and particles can settle in it, it is usually not necessary to sand between coats.

Shellac is a resinous finish made from lac, a substance deposited by the female lac beetle on the limbs of various trees in southern Asia.

Polyurethane is a durable, polymer-based finish. It requires paint thinner or mineral spirits for cleanup.

*Paper is a gracious and versatile material, easily transformed through folding, cutting, tearing, or painting, and a wonderful medium for creating the warm and inviting atmosphere that we all desire in our homes. The timeless quality of paper makes it the perfect complement to any decorating scheme, traditional or contemporary. Whether crisp, clean rice paper is used to evoke the elegance of traditional Asian homes or paper sconces reinvent the flair of a chic urban restaurant, paper accents give your home a look that can be simultaneously ethereal, environmentally friendly, and earthy.*

# PAPER LIVING ROOM

*In this chapter, silk-screened Asian papers redefine the surface of a simple wooden chair and transform it into "art" furniture. Highly textured abaca-fiber paper is torn and layered to decorate a clay vessel; and as has long been done in Korea, paper can even be used underfoot, as shown in the exotic decoupaged floor cloths.*

*The effects that can be achieved with paper are infinite; the only limit is your imagination. Because paper is accessible, affordable, and flexible, you can feel free to learn by experiment and trial and error. If you haven't used paper much for design, start with something small. Perhaps it's your first time setting up a Christmas tree and you haven't built an ornament collection yet. Use paper. Make paper chains from origami papers, cut snowflakes from handmade paper, shred shiny gift wrap to make tinsel. Your tree will be stunning, and you will begin to see the decorative possibilities of this fabulous material.*

## MATERIALS

- wooden chair

- medium/coarse grade sandpaper

- acrylic wood primer (if the
  chair is unfinished)

- assorted lightweight papers
  printed with Asian lettering or
  foreign-language newspapers

- decoupage medium or
  white glue

- scissors

- acrylic oak stain

- cotton rags

- disposable sponge brushes

# LAYERED PAPER CHAIR

*Create an exotic piece of furniture by covering the entire surface of a chair with cut pieces of decorative papers. The papered piece is finished with a dark stain to highlight its structure and to give it character. In this example, we used an assortment of handmade papers with Asian symbols and drawings, but you can easily substitute pages of a foreign-language newspaper to achieve a similar look. This is a sturdy wooden dining chair from the 1930s, purchased for a few dollars at a junk shop. It's a nice example of the type of chair you should seek out for a project like this. It has many wide, flat surfaces, which are perfect for layering with paper, and just enough details to make it interesting without the added challenge of working around too many odd, rounded angles. Though your chair will look like a piece of art when it's finished, it will have a very strong finish that will stand up fine to any normal use—so sit down and enjoy.*

# 1

# LAYERED PAPER CHAIR

**STEP 1** Choose your papers. Cut several squares and rectangles of each, ranging in size from 1 to 4 inches (3 cm to 10 cm) long and wide. Next, prepare the chair. For a chair that has been previously painted or varnished, clean thoroughly with soap and water, using a cloth or scrub brush. Sand the surface with coarse sandpaper, then wipe with a damp cloth to remove any dust. For a new chair, seal any holes or cracks with a wood filler, then sand the surface with medium sandpaper. Coat once with acrylic wood primer.

**STEP 2** Using a sponge brush, begin layering pieces of paper over the chair. Coat the back of the paper piece entirely with decoupage glue and lay it on. Then, smooth over the paper again with the brush to push out any air bubbles and to coat the top of it with glue. As you add additional pieces, overlap the edges of the previous ones you laid down. For a uniform look, apply all the papers so that the edges square with the vertical and horizontal lines of the chair. Use certain colored papers to accent particular areas of the chair: I used a black paper on the underside of the seat and on the lower crossbar. I used orange paper to highlight a detail of the leg. Experiment as you go, and if you want to change a particular area midstream, just add a new layer of paper on top. Once you are pleased with the arrangement of the papers, let dry overnight.

**FINISHING TOUCH** To complete the chair, use a soft cloth and diluted acrylic oak stain to darken the chair. First, lightly drag the cloth along all the edges, not the flat surfaces. Add just a little stain at a time all over until you start to see how it looks, then go back and darken as much as you wish until you are pleased with the surface.
You may also want to slightly darken the entire surface over the papers. To test this, start in an inconspicuous place with very diluted stain and experiment until you determine the shade you want to achieve. When the staining is completed, let the chair dry completely. With a new sponge brush, add several coats of decoupage medium or a satin acrylic varnish to finish and protect the surface.

- 3 sheets of handmade paper in marine, ocher, and persimmon

- collage glue

- metal ruler

- paintbrush

- paper clay

- acrylic paints to match the papers

- raffia

- skewer or nail

# PAPER-COVERED OLIVE JAR

*Paper can be laminated onto nearly any surface; clay works especially well. In this project, an old olive jar is spiced up using a Caribbean palette of papers. The papers were torn into strips to leave a soft edge and applied to the jar leaving small spaces in between to allow some of the natural clay color to show through. The beads were formed out of commercially available paper clay, which is essentially powdered paper pulp mixed with a glue binder. It feels like clay and dries to a solid form. Another alternative is to shape the beads out of papier-mâché mix. Papier-mâché is a French term meaning "chewed paper." The mix is merely a powdered paper pulp that, when combined with water, can be molded or sculpted into any shape. This project features olive-shaped beads that were painted with colorful stripes and strung onto raffia to provide the final accent.*

# PAPER-COVERED OLIVE JAR

**STEP 1**   Tear strips from each color of paper that range in width from 1/2" to 1 1/2" (1 cm to 4 cm). To tear a strip, align a metal ruler along the line to be torn; then, holding the paper from the top corner with your fingers, pull up and across the ruler's edge. Starting at the bottom of the vase, begin adding strips of paper. Brush the glue onto the entire back of the paper, then lay the strip onto the jar. Use your fingers to smooth out any wrinkles in the paper and to ease the paper around the jar. Alternating colors and sizes, cover the entire jar up to the neck and let dry.

**STEP 2**   Use paper clay to mold two olive-shaped beads. Roll a ball of clay between the palms of your hand, and then give a few extra rolls in the same direction to create the olive shape. Repeat to make a second bead. Pierce the clay with a skewer or nail and let dry completely.

3

**STEP 3** Use acrylic paint and coat the beads in a base color. Paint simple stripes over the base color in another color. Apply a coat of acrylic sealer and let dry. String the beads onto a few strands of raffia, knot the ends to hold the beads, and tie the raffia around the neck of the jar.

## VARIATION

Change the directions of your stripes to accentuate the shape of your object. For this rounded jar; the paper strips need to be tapered a bit at the top and bottom so that they line up properly. Just tear the strips with a ruler; then do the tapering by hand. Tie three big beads choker-style around the neck for a different decorative finish. This technique would work well on any terra-cotta item.

## MATERIALS

- 13" x 15" (33 cm x 38 cm) paper-laminated chicken wire sheet

- battery-operated floral lights

- paper flowers

- burnt umber, burnt sienna, and warm yellow acrylic paint

- old toothbrush

- acrylic medium

- wire cutters

- work gloves

- hot glue gun

- tape measure

- hanging hook

# PAPER FLOWER SCONCES

*Use paper strengthened with wire mesh to create these illuminated sconces. The construction is simple; all you do is roll a rectangular sheet into a cone. You can purchase paper with wire already embedded or make your own. To make your own, bend your wire into the desired shape, then measure and wrap a sheet of paper around the form. Coat the entire structure with acrylic medium to bind the paper and wire together. The sconce is decorated with a simple splatter-painting technique. If you are making your own wire-laminated paper, do the spatter painting first, then adhere the decorated paper around the wire with acrylic medium. The flowers shown here are also made of paper. See the Variation on page 21 to learn how to make your own paper flowers.*

# PAPER FLOWER SCONCES

**STEP 1**   With the wire side down, use a tooth-brush and diluted acrylic paint to create a splatter pattern on your paper. Dip the brush in your paint, then riffle the bristles to release a fine spray. Experiment on scrap paper to test the paint effect, then move to your project paper. Let the paper dry. Wearing gloves, cut a 13" x 15" (33 cm x 38 cm) piece of wire-backed paper.

**STEP 2**   Lay the sheet flat with the wire facing up. Again wearing gloves, fold in each edge 1/2" (1 cm) to create a hem.

**STEP 3** Roll the sheet into a cone and hot glue the edges together. Coat the outside of the cone with acrylic varnish. Let dry completely, then add another coat of varnish.

**STEP 4** Test-fit your flowers in the sconce and trim the stems as needed. Remove the flowers and wrap the stems with floral lights. Place the bouquet into the interior of the cone. Add a small hanging hook to the back to display the sconce. Plug in the batteries as needed when you want the illumination.

## VARIATION

To make a basic paper flower, cut a 1 ½" x 12" (4 cm x 30 cm) strip of medium-weight handmade paper. Crumple and uncrumple the paper strip a few times to soften it and give it texture. With a knotted thread, sew a small running stitch ½" (1 cm) in from one side along the strip. When you get to the end, gently slide the paper down the thread until it is half the original length. Knot the other end of the thread to secure. Roll the gathered side around a piece of floral wire to shape your flower head. Put a dab of glue at the base of the roll to secure. Then wrap the base of the paper flower and the wire stem with floral tape.

# ASIAN PAPER FLORM MAT

## MATERIALS

- 38" x 28" (97 cm x 71 cm) cotton canvas
- assortment of four decorative Asian papers for the background
- paper with a central motif (Sources for this include postcards, calendars, and greeting cards.)
- PVA glue
- acrylic primer
- burnt umber acrylic paint
- burnt umber artist's oil paint
- polyurethane varnish
- disposable sponge brushes
- roller
- scissors
- ruler or measuring tape

*Use your favorite Asian papers on the floor by laminating them to a sturdy canvas base. Choose a light- to medium-weight paper that will easily absorb the diluted PVA glue and adhere well to the canvas surface. For a free-form look, layer your papers into an interesting collage. For a more modern piece, create a tiled look using same-size squares. This version was inspired by Asian wall hangings that juxtapose and layer rectangular shapes. A wash of burnt umber paint was used to give the patina of age.*

# ASIAN PAPER FLOOR MAT

**STEP 1**  Measure and cut a 38" x 28" (97 cm x 71 cm) piece of canvas. Use a roller to apply one coat of acrylic primer. Let dry.

**STEP 2**  Plan the arrangement of your paper design. Cut out each shape and set aside. Thin PVA glue with water (one part glue to one part water) and adhere each sheet to the canvas, starting with the bottom layer. Use the palm of your hand to gently smooth out all the papers, starting in the center and working any air bubbles out and off the edges. Let dry thoroughly.

**STEP 3** Dilute burnt umber acrylic with water and apply a wash to the papered canvas using a sponge brush. If the paint wash is too dark, you can use a paper towel to blot off any excess paint.

**STEP 4** Add a few drops burnt umber artist's oil paint to the polyurethane. Apply a thin coat to your papered mat using a sponge brush. Let dry completely. Lightly sand with fine sandpaper. Wipe away any dust with a damp cloth. Repeat to add a minimum of three coats, sanding between each, and applying the brush strokes of each layer in the opposite direction.

## VARIATION

For a quicker small rug, use a single sheet for the central motif of your design and just add a border. Here, I used a paper printed with animals. The edging is made from a paper border created with printed newsprint. Make your own newsprint border paper by cutting newspapers into 5" (13 cm) strips and gluing them end to end. Run a sponge brush loaded with acrylic paint along both edges of the strip. Then, print a pattern along the length using your favorite stamp. Each corner is finished with a handmade tassel.

*The exquisite pairing of paper and light can transform the windows of your home in subtle and unique ways. Before choosing paper for a window treatment, hold it up to various light sources to examine its translucency and the way it changes under different conditions.*

*This chapter will present four techniques for using paper as a window treatment. The first project shows how to compose window streamers built from stacked paper shapes delineated by lengths of straw.*

# PAPER WINDOWS

*These streamers can add personality to an otherwise simple room by playing with reflected light and shadows. For a more refined window treatment, Thai lace papers can be shaped and hung from curtain clips to disguise an unwanted view without obscuring much-wanted light. Also, you'll learn how to construct a simple accordion-fold paper shade that can be delightfully enhanced with dimensional kirigami folds.*

*You'll also learn two techniques for applying paper to glass. For complete privacy, you can cover actual windowpanes with paper, or cover a salvaged window that can be transported as needed to any location. For an impermanent application, the trick is using egg whites! The paper can be changed or removed at any future time by merely soaking it off with a wet sponge. These techniques highlight the intrinsic beauty of the papers used while still allowing light to penetrate and grace a room.*

## MATERIALS

- 2 sheets medium-weight decorative seafoam-colored paper (approximately 26" x 38" (66 cm x 97 cm)

- 2 sheets white corrugated board

- 1 box clear plastic drinking straws

- 1 ball of white cotton string

- 1 wooden dowel or curtain rod to fit your window

- wood stain for the dowel if desired

- scissors

- embroidery or large sewing needle

*(These materials make seven 40" [101 cm] streamers that fill the length of a 36" [91 cm] dowel.)*

# PAPER-SHAPE WINDOW STREAMERS

*These streamers provide a playful and geometric window design that will cast great shadows when the sun is out. Depending on the papers you choose, the streamers can be very neutral or very colorful. Use them to disguise a less-than-scenic view or to soften the light from a bright window. They are constructed with stacks of paper and corrugated board shapes that float on strings between short lengths of drinking straws.*

# PAPER-SHAPE WINDOW STREAMERS

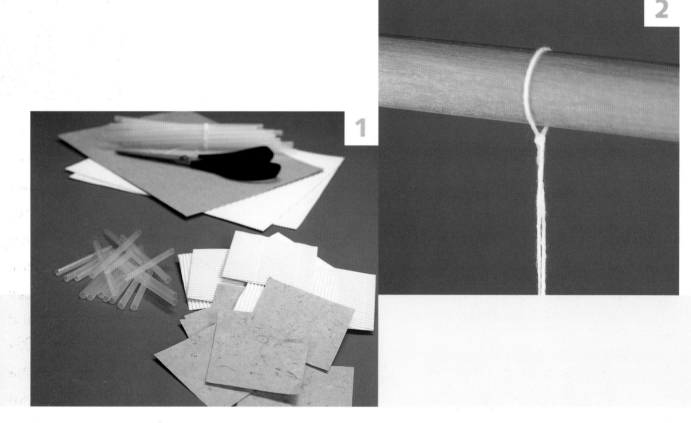

**STEP 1** Cut both sheets of colored paper into irregular quadrilateral shapes. Cut white corrugated board in the same fashion. Cut drinking straws into thirds at slightly irregular lengths. Cut all the ends of the straws at a slant. (I used four 3 1/2" (9 cm) and fourteen 2 1/2" (6 cm) lengths of straw for each streamer, varying the sequence of long and short straw lengths as I strung each strand.) Cut a length of cotton string equal to twice the height of your window, plus 10" (25 cm) for tying off. Plan for one streamer every 4" (10 cm) across the width of your window.

**STEP 2** Tie the string around the dowel, knotting below it, and leaving two equal-length strands. Slide both strands through a needle. Drop the needle through a piece of cut straw. Slide the straw up to the dowel to hide the knot.

When you cut the straws, don't try to cut them straight across, or the paper sections will be at an exact ninety-degree angle, causing the streamers to look very thin because you only see the papers' edges. Instead, cut the straws at a slight angle. You will see more of the papers' surface area, and this adds to the asymmetrical look of the paper shapes.

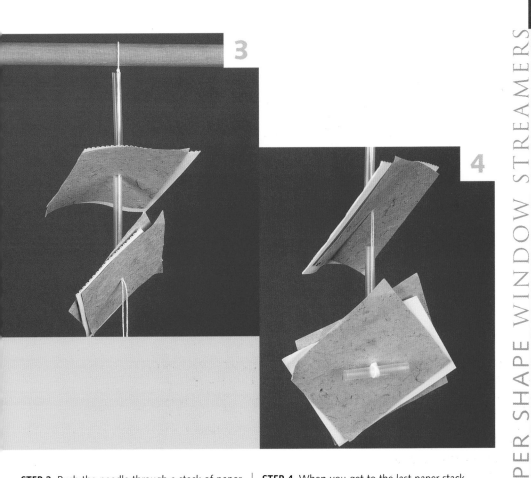

PAPER SHAPE WINDOW STREAMERS

## VARIATION

Use an earthy mauve paper combined with wavy corrugated board for a different palette and look. This paper has a combination of deep maroon fibers with lots of neutral color fibers mixed in, making a soft mauve sheet overall. The neutral fibers helped tie in the natural color of the wavy corrugated board. For even more pizzazz, try adding glass beads above and below each length of straw in your streamers.

**STEP 3** Push the needle through a stack of paper and corrugated board. (A stack can consist of one paper and one corrugated shape or two papers with a corrugated shape in between. Alternate two- and three-layer stacks as you go.) Follow with another length of straw. Continue threading paper stacks and straws onto the string until you reach the desired length.

**STEP 4** When you get to the last paper stack, remove the needle. Lay a straw underneath the stack between the two pieces of string. Knot the two ends around the straw, then thread the ends back up through the last needle hole. Sandwich them between the layered papers and trim any excess. Repeat steps one through four to make more streamers.

## MATERIALS

- 24" x 36" (61 cm x 91 cm) sheet white Thai "horizontal lace" paper (foreground paper)

- 1 similarly sized sheet aqua Indian cotton rag paper (background paper)

- 5 metal curtain clips and rings

- 1 curtain rod or dowel

- 10 white silk or paper leaves

- lengths of silk ribbon or cord (optional, see step 3)

- scissors

- white craft glue

- craft paper (to make pattern)

# ARCHED WINDOW LUMINARY

*Create this graceful window treatment by hanging two styles of paper together for a layered effect—an aqua-colored, Indian rag paper and a white Thai lace paper with a horizontal pattern. A pointed archway is trimmed out of the aqua background paper, allowing an elegant space for sunlight to filter through the lace paper that hangs in front. The papers are hung together with silver curtain clips, with silk leaves added for a finishing touch.*

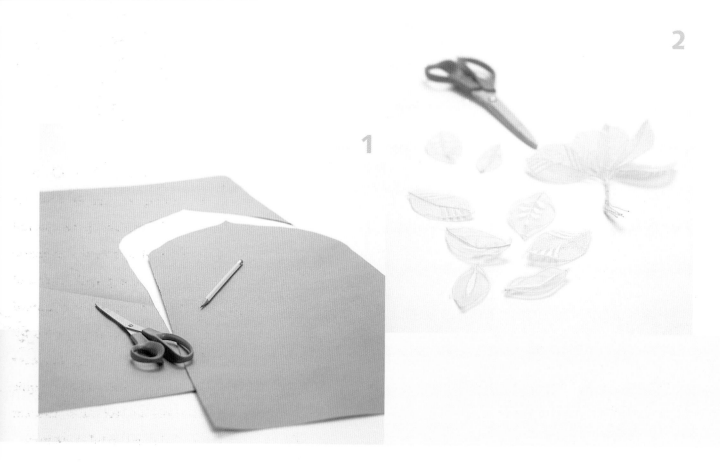

**STEP 1** Trim the background paper to the same size as the lace paper. Lay the craft paper on a flat surface and cut out an arch pattern. Trace the arch shape with a pencil, centered, onto the back side of the background paper. Carefully cut arch pattern from background paper.

**STEP 2** Prepare the leaves by trimming each from the twisted wire stem. If you can't locate silk leaves (commonly available in bridal and craft stores), try making your own by tracing out the shape of a real leaf onto rice or other handmade paper and cutting out the shapes. Here, a large and a small leaf are paired for decorative effect.

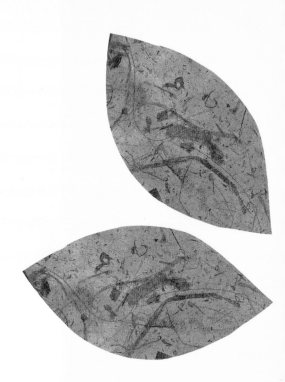

## TIPS

- Before purchasing materials, measure the window and decide whether the curtain will hang inside or outside the frame. You'll need more paper for an outside-mounted curtain.

- If the paper you like is too narrow or short, carefully piece together several sheets by stitching or ironing "invisible seam" fusible webbing with an iron set on "low."

- Don't use paper window panels near the oven or a heat source of any kind. Try pairing a paper valance with simple wooden shutters if the window is next to the stove.

- Substitute any lightweight, pliable papers for those listed. Avoid stiff or heavy papers; they won't hang nicely and the translucent effect of light will be lost.

**3**

**4**

## VARIATION

Try cutting leaf shapes from the excess background paper instead of using white silk: this technique creates a more graphic look and highlights the underlayer of colored paper. Many other shapes will work as well. For a celestial look, a navy blue paper underlayer looks terrific with yellow stars and crescent embellishments added to the front.

**STEP 3** Position the silk leaves, pairing a single large leaf with a small one, then affix together with a dot of glue and let dry. Attach the rings to the curtain clips. If you would like the leaves to hang loose and move with currents of air, braid the desired lengths of silken cord or ribbon and affix leaves to the end with a few stitches.

**STEP 4** Lay both sheets together, right side up. Spacing evenly, clip papers together, catching the leaves along the top border. Run a curtain rod or dowel through the rings and hang as desired.

ARCHED WINDOW LUMINARY

- lightweight translucent paper

- assorted dried flowers (or substitute paper embedded with botanicals for the items above)

- metal ruler

- craft knife

- cutting mat

- acrylic matte medium

- disposable sponge brush

- repositionable spray adhesive

- window cleaner

- paper towels

# PAPERED WINDOW SASH
# WITH FLOWER PETALS

*Rescue an old window sash from a flea market (or perhaps even your own basement) and create a lovely display. This is a wonderful way to show off beautiful papers, to soften the light coming into a room, or to filter light for sun-sensitive plants. Use it to add an architectural element to a room, or to provide a decorative screen front of an existing window or glass door. You could treat your sash like any piece of framed art; position it over a mantel or use it as a backdrop for other collectibles.*

**STEP 1** Prepare all your materials. Dry several flowers' heads between the pages of a heavy book. (This should be done a week or two in advance so the flowers are completely dry before you start.) Clean the glass panes on both sides with paper towels and glass cleaner. Measure each section of glass on the window. If you are using an unusual window with odd-shaped panes for your project, make pattern pieces to fit as you size your papers. Use a ruler, cutting mat, and craft knife to cut paper pieces to fit each pane of glass. For softer edges, tear the paper instead by pulling it up gently against the edge of the ruler. To add your own botanicals to the paper, first plan your arrangement on the paper. Then, lay all the botanicals face down over newsprint. Spray them lightly with spray adhesive, then carefully re-create your arrangement on the paper, gently tapping the flowers into place to hold them. Finish preparing the paper for each pane of your window.

Cut paper snowflakes from beautiful translucent papers and adhere them with an egg white mixture to your windows over the holidays. When the season is over, just sponge them off. Add paper flowers in the springtime, and paper leaf shapes for fall.

**2**

## PAPERED WINDOW SASH WITH FLOWER PETALS

### VARIATION

You can use this technique on the existing windows in your home. Simply substitute egg white for the acrylic matte medium. It will adhere the paper to the window, but will easily wash off with warm water and a sponge whenever you want to remove it or change to another style of paper. (You won't be able to reuse the paper.) To mount paper on an existing clean window, paint the window first with the egg white, then lay your paper over the top and smooth it on using the brush or your hands. This is a great alternative to shades or blinds, and allows you to disguise an unpleasant view without losing all the light. The window shown here features Queen Anne's lace layered with a thin yellow paper with lots of visible fibers.

**STEP 2** Lay the window onto your work surface with the front side of the window facing down. You will add the papers to the backside of the glass. Using a sponge brush, coat the first pane of glass with acrylic matte medium. (The acrylic matte medium looks milky when first applied but dries to a clear finish and will make your paper more translucent.) Place the paper face down on top of the wet glass. Use the sponge brush to smooth the paper onto the glass and to brush any air bubbles out the edges. If necessary, add a little more acrylic matte medium from the back so that the entire paper is evenly coated. If you have an air bubble that you can't brush out, use your craft knife to cut a tiny puncture in the center of it, then ease the air out and tamp the paper flat with the sponge brush. Repeat to cover each pane with paper. Let dry.

## MATERIALS

- medium-weight Japanese printed paper
- cotton waxed cord
- bone beads
- scissors
- craft knife
- cutting mat
- cardboard or mat board
- PVA glue
- bone folder
- hole punch
- clear hole reinforcers
- metal ruler
- pencil

# KIRIGAMI ACCORDION SHADE

*Create this elegant window valance by combining an accordion fold with simple kirigami mountain- and valley-folds that add interest to the surface. Kirigami is a Japanese paper craft that incorporates cuts and folds to transform two-dimensional papers into three-dimensional designs. Here, some simple cuts are made perpendicular to the accordion folds. When the paper between the cuts is folded in the opposite direction, you create a whimsical pattern of shapes that pop from the surface. This decorative valance is a nice way to top off a window that you don't necessarily need to completely cover, one where you want to enjoy the view, such as a small kitchen window with a view to the garden that you enjoy. The pattern is easy to adapt for a larger window by gluing two or more sheets of paper together. To begin, you will need to measure your window to determine the desired width of your valance. Trim your paper accordingly, and remember that the valance should fit easily within the window frame with at least a half-inch (1 cm) of space on each side so it can slide freely.*

# KIRIGAMI ACCORDIAN SHADE

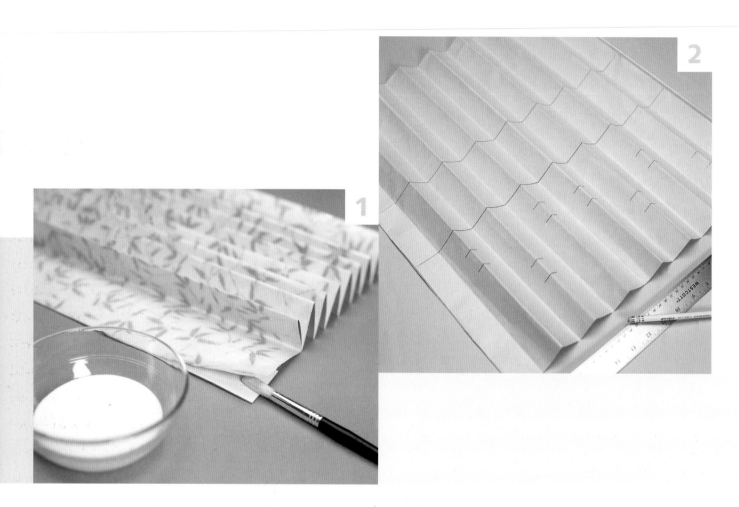

**STEP 1** Crease the paper into accordion folds with the width of each pleat staying constant at around 1 ¹/₂" (4 cm). Use a bone folder to press the creases smooth at each fold. Reinforce the top and the bottom of the shade with a strip of stiff cardboard or mat board. Conceal the board between two folds of the paper.

**STEP 2** Open the paper flat with the front pattern facing down. From that perspective, the accordion folds will appear alternately as mountain- and valley-folds; the mountains are those that rise up and the valleys are those folds that recede. Using a pencil, mark off a strip 4" (10 cm) wide down the center of the paper perpendicular to the folds. You will not make any kirigami cuts in this area. Next, draw several pairs of short parallel lines over the surface of the paper, with approximately six to eight pairs on each side of the fold. Each pair of parallel lines should be 1" (3 cm) apart and should run perpendicular to the accordion folds. Each pair of parallel lines should start at a valley fold, cross one mountain fold, and end at the next valley fold. Using a craft knife, ruler, and cutting mat, cut along your marked lines. When you are finished, fold the paper between each set of lines in the opposite direction.

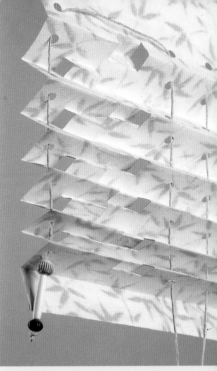

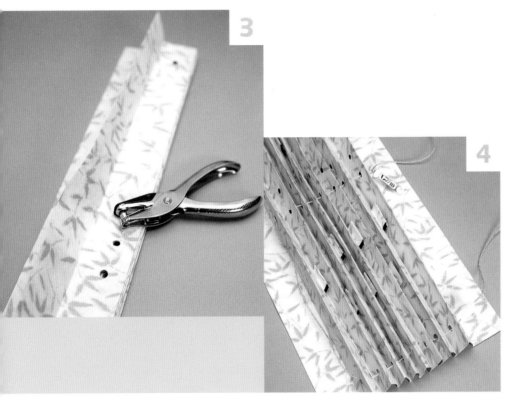

**STEP 3** Punch holes along each side of the valance, and punch another two rows, centered in the middle of the shade and 1" (3 cm) apart. All holes should be centered within the creases. Add a layer of reinforcement rings to all the holes.

**STEP 4** Thread waxed cord up through the holes in the left side of the valance to the top, leaving extra cord hanging from the bottom. Next, thread the cord down through the left middle row. Once you reach the bottom of the shade, thread on a series of decorative bone beads, loop around the bottom bead and then thread the cord back up through the rest of the beads. Tie an overhand knot at the top of the beaded strand. Thread the cord up through the right middle row to the top, leaving the beads handing down in the center of the shade. Finally, thread down through the right side.

**STEP 5** Slide open the valance to its loosest position. Thread a series of bone beads onto the cords hanging out the two bottom corners of the valance. Make a knot below each bead strand to secure the beads and trim off the end of the cord. To work the valance, pull on both side strands to draw the shade up. To close, or loosen, the shade, pull the center bead strand gently downward.

## VARIATION

To add interest, you can create kirigami folds that fold in and out in both directions. To create a fold that pops back, mark the set of parallel lines to start and end at a mountain fold and cross one valley fold (and remember, this is while you are working from the back of the shade). To accentuate the cut areas, lay a contrasting paper over the reverse-folded sections.

*In the heart of the home, the kitchen, paper is the perfect material to complement the activities of cooking, eating, gathering, and entertaining. This chapter explores several projects that introduce you to tearing, tiling, and layering paper to create a decorative table runner and coasters, a stylish bistro tray, and a colorful spice rack.*

*You'll also find several ideas for using paper to decorate for special events. Whether you're planning for a wedding or shower, a special birthday, creating a centerpiece, or delicately wrapping the contents*

# PAPER KITCHEN

*of a gift basket, paper can evoke the perfect mood. Delicate metallic papers and unusual rayon "lace" papers become paper cone favors, crisp napkin rings, and translucent votive covers that can be used to accessorize a splendid wedding celebration. Mexican paper cut place mats are a fun and simple way to add zest to a party, or try using textured cotton rag papers to mold a subtle yet dramatic centerpiece bowl. Carefully folded colorful wax papers become a gracious and yet utilitarian way to package gifts of food, revealing the thought that went into selecting something special.*

*Many of the paper accessories featured here can easily double as portable party favors, small but beautiful tokens, made by hand with care. Paper is the perfect choice for a gathering where you want to add special touches that are at once easy to achieve and yet beautiful, festive, or elegant.*

## MATERIALS

- 5' x 15" (1.5 m x 38 cm) piece strong parchment for the base

- 3 ½' x 12" (1.1 m x 30 cm) piece of handmade paper

- 3' x 10' (.9 m x 3 m) piece handmade paper

- metal ruler

- liquid laminate

- disposable sponge brush

- waxed paper

# PAPER TABLECLOTH

*Here, a delicate but very strong parchment paper acts as the base for a willowy table runner. Two layers of contrasting papers are bonded to the central surface area using a liquid laminate. The rough pattern of maroon strips is torn from a single sheet of paper with the pieces laid side by side in order to form the top layer. When the laminate dries, the surface becomes water repellent. The fringed sides add a touch of whimsy. Use this runner along a dining table or sideboard, or lay it out as a scarf for a dresser or a hall table with the fringes left to cascade off the sides.*

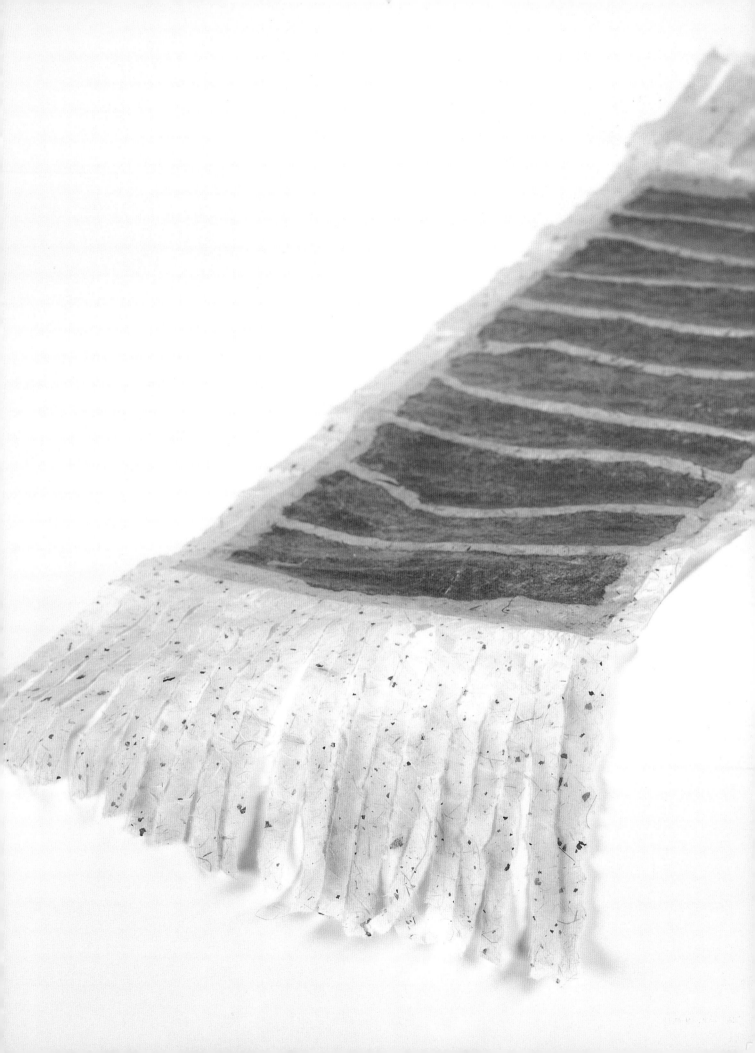

# PAPER TABLECLOTH

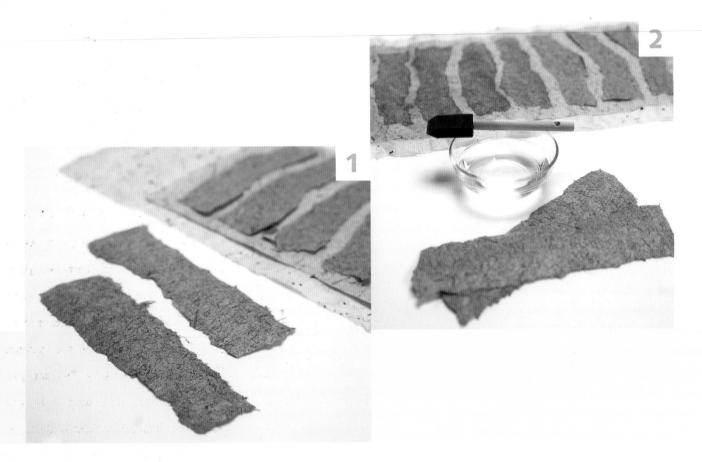

**STEP 1** Measure and prepare three sheets of different papers for your runner. You can cut or tear the edges depending on the look you want. Use the strongest paper as your base. Once complete, lay the top sheet in front of you and begin tearing it slowly into ragged strips. Leave the strips in place as you move across the sheet.

**STEP 2** Working on a waxed paper-protected surface, coat the bottom sheet with a thin layer of liquid laminate. Add the torn strips from the second 3 1/2" x 12" (1.1 m x 30.5 cm) piece of handmade paper, centered on top. Begin to laminate the strips over the top of the second sheet, leaving approximately 1" (3 cm) between each strip. Let dry.

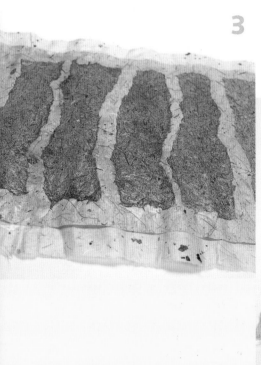

3

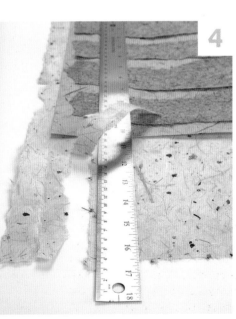

4

## VARIATION

Use this same technique to create matching coasters from your paper scraps. Just layer a two-color background and add an arrangement of torn squares for the pattern. Depending on the colors you use, your strips and squares may look like animal prints. Coat all the layers with liquid laminate and let them dry completely. Set the coasters in the pages of a book for an hour or so to flatten them before you set them out for use.

**STEP 3** Paint the layered area of the runner with another coat of liquid laminate and let dry. Don't coat the area that will become the fringe.

**STEP 4** Tear the fringe using a metal ruler. Hold ruler in one hand and pull up the paper with opposite fingers to tear. Make each fringe approximately 1" (3 cm) wide. Because the paper is strong, you will need to tear carefully to keep the fringe intact. It's easiest to tear only a little of the strip at a time.

- unfinished pine tray

- white acrylic stain

- medium size paintbrush (for stain)

- cloth or paper to cover work surface

- 1 sheet Barcelona white cotton rag paper

- 1 sheet lilac drawing paper

- 1 sheet Thai spiral lace paper

- decoupage medium

- metal ruler

- scissors

- pencil

# PAPER TILE BISTRO TRAY

*Stack and glue coordinating paper squares to make tiles for the surface of a wooden serving tray or any unfinished wooden item. The tray is coated with a translucent white acrylic stain that allows the grain of the wood to show through. Each tile is made by layering the paper with a simple decoupage medium, which also works as a glue. Once all the tiles are completed, several coats of the same medium seal the tiles to the tray surface.*

# PAPER TILE BISTRO TRAY

**STEP 1** Using a sponge brush, evenly coat the pine tray with acrylic white stain and let dry. It is easiest to begin with the inner area of the tray, then turn it over and paint the exterior, as shown. Acrylic dries quickly, so paint carefully and correct any drips immediately. Extremely porous wood may require a second coat.

**STEP 2** Measure the interior dimensions of the tray bottom. Use these dimensions as a guide to the largest size paper squares you will need. Here, the tray bottom was divided into six segments of equal size. Create graduated squares from each of the three papers using scissors, or, for a natural edge, by tearing along the edge of a metal ruler. You might also choose to line the tray bottom with a sheet of paper and then sprinkle small paper tiles on top, for a "confetti" effect.

## TIPS

- For an icy or matte look, add a layer of vellum or white tissue paper and then seal with decoupage medium or "paint" with colored tissue paper on tiles by wetting small pieces with glue and brushing onto the surface of the tile. Layer edges or hues (yellow over blue, for example) to mix colors.

- Add pretty texture by using a needle to pierce geometric patterns in the topmost paper squares before layering tiles.

- You may want to sand the tray lightly to smooth the surface before you begin. To be sure tiles will lay out symmetrically, cut some plain paper to the same size planned for the tiles and lay it over the tray. Adjustments are then very simple to make—before you have cut the beautiful paper you have made or purchased for the tiles.

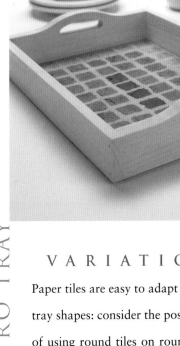

## VARIATION

Paper tiles are easy to adapt to many tray shapes: consider the possibilities of using round tiles on round trays, triangles on any shape, or tiny squares in gradually deepening hues—as in this variation. Another way to change the look and feel of this project is to tear, rather than cut, tile shapes. Tearing softens the edge of the tile and beautifully highlights the fiber and grain of the paper.

**STEP 3** Make tiles by gluing the graduated squares of paper together using decoupage medium. It is best to dab glue on each square with a tapping motion rather than trying to evenly coat the whole tile. Dabbing will help keep the paper from warping; so will covering the tiles with a weight or heavy book as they dry. Let the tiles dry for at least an hour before applying them to tray surface.

**STEP 4** Adhere tiles to tray surface with decoupage medium, then add two very light coats over the top of the tiles to seal.

## MATERIALS

- wooden display case with shelves
- coordinating medium-weight textured paper in three colors
- 4 sheets of coordinating origami paper
- collage glue
- small sponge brush
- scissors
- metal ruler
- pencil
- waxed cotton cord
- hammer
- 4 small nails

# PAPERED SPICE CASE

*Use paper to cover a simple wooden display case and turn it into a cozy rack for spices. This cabinet features origami papers for the background and uses a medium-weight highly textured paper to cover the exterior and the shelves. Although all the colors are different, they are all from a warm palette so they work together nicely and go with the warm-toned spices that they house. To secure the contents of each shelf, braid waxed cotton cord and string it across each opening.*

# PAPERED SPICE CASE

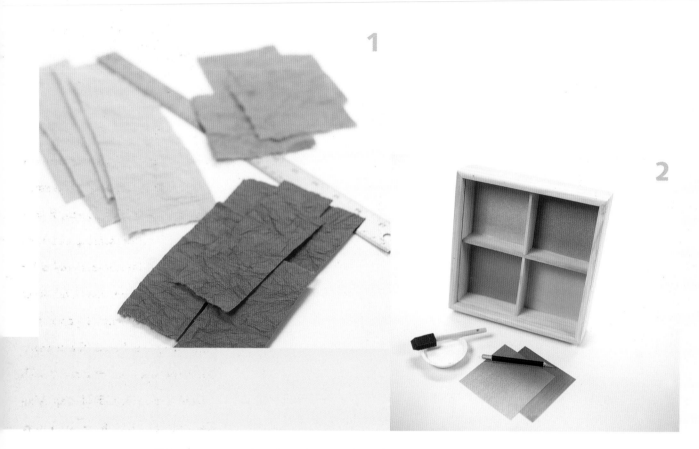

**STEP 1** Measure, mark, and tear the papers for each section of the box according to the measurements of your wooden case. Use a different color for the inside dividers, the inside rim, and the outside rim. Tear, rather than cut, the paper along the lines. Firmly hold a metal ruler along one of your marks, then pull the paper up and towards you. This will give your papers a softer edge, which is more easily blended along a seam.

**STEP 2** Measure, mark, and cut the sheets of origami paper for the back wall. Use a small sponge brush and collage glue to adhere the papers to the case. Smooth the papers from the center out to press out any air bubbles.

Apply a thin layer of acrylic varnish or decoupage medium over the paper, if desired. This will create a more translucent effect and give the paper a sheen while also protecting it. A varnish will likely darken the color of your paper, so keep this in mind when you are choosing your colors. If you don't choose to put a finish coat on the paper, it will retain its matte appearance.

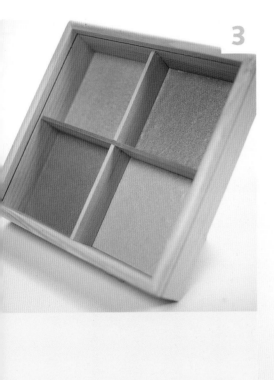

**3**

**4**

PAPERED SPICE CASE

# V A R I A T I O N

Here, the case is used as a memory holder. Rather than using origami papers for the background, it was covered with the same paper used on the sides. We chose a cool color palette, and then tore and inset coordinating squares of paper over each background area. White paper roses and buds were attached with hot glue, but instead of displaying flowers, you can chose to feature other personal mementos such as seashells, seedpods, or memorabilia from your travels.

**STEP 3** To glue a sheet of paper, use a sponge brush to apply a thin layer of collage glue on the back of the paper and then place the paper in the appropriate area. Use a toothpick to position the paper evenly into the corners and along the straight edges of the wood. Use bits of torn paper to patch up any bare spots. Paper the inside dividers first; then cover the inside area of the rim. Finish by covering the outside rim of the case.

**STEP 4** Cut three lengths of waxed cotton cord that are three times the width of your shelf. Make an overhand knot in one end, then braid the three strands to the desired length. Tie another overhand knot to secure the braid. Cut off any excess cord 1" (3 cm) from the knot on each end. Repeat to make a braid for each shelf. Lay one braid across the case approximately 1" (3 cm) above the shelf. Gently hammer a small nail into each knot, centering the nail in the edge of the wood. Repeat to attach each braided cord. Now your shelf is ready to hang and fill with spice jars.

## MATERIALS

- rayon paper scraps
- lavender handmade paper
- heart-shaped doilies
- ribbon
- paper clay
- initial and heart rubber stamps
- stamp ink
- embossing powders
- double-sided tape
- craft knife
- acrylic matte medium

*Whether you're preparing a lavish wedding or a cozy wedding shower for a friend, paper is the perfect accent for a pretty affair.*

# PAPER WEDDING FAVORS

- To make a paper cone, cut a square that will accommodate a heart-shaped doily. Lay the heart doily so that the point of the heart rests in a corner of the square. Stamp a tiny heart in the corner opposite the doily's point. Turn the papers over and roll into

- Use translucent printed rayon papers to add a paper cuff to tiny glass votives. Cut the strips to size and wrap them around the votive. To adhere them to the glass, brush acrylic matte medium over the paper cuff and let dry.

- Make paper napkin rings using the same papers. Layer the strips and attach the ends with double-sided tape.

- Create a wine glass tag that doubles as a place card. Use a paper clay mix to form some clay. Roll out the clay into a 1/8" (.3 cm) inch sheet between waxed paper sheets. Use a craft knife to carve the clay sheet into 1" (3 cm) squares. Use an inked rubber stamp to impress each square with the initial of the guest. Enhance the stamp with embossing powder and activate using a heat tool. Let the tile dry, then adhere to a white stationery tag with white glue. Tie the initial tag to the wine glass stem with ribbon.

*Paper bowls make beautiful presentation vessels. Here, the large bowl was molded over an African basket and the small bowls were molded over apples. You can use a rounded item of virtually any size to cast a bowl.*

## MATERIALS

- textured brown cotton paper
- medium-weight colored hand-made paper
- bowls and apples for molds
- PVA glue
- aluminum foil
- petroleum jelly
- acrylic paint

# PAPER CENTERPIECE BOWLS

Cover the basket entirely in foil, and then coat it with a layer of petroleum jelly. This will help release the molded paper. A brown cotton paper that was soft, pliable, and had the look of aged and wrinkled leather was used to mold the large bowl and a deep teal sheet was used for the leaf-shaped accents. Cut five leaf shapes. Wet and then lay them over the foil first. Next, cover the entire basket with wet torn pieces of paper, no larger than 3" (8 cm) in any direction, overlapping as you go. Mix a solution of 1 teaspoon of PVA glue to one cup of water to wet the paper pieces. Make more solution as needed. For a sturdy container, build up several layers of torn paper until you feel the thickness is sufficient. Let each layer dry before adding another.

Molding two circles of wet paper around an apple makes a small bowl. To start, choose a mixing bowl with a rim diameter of about 8" (20 cm). Place the bowl rim down over a sheet of handmade paper. Tear away the paper around the rim until you are left with an 8" (20 cm) circle. Repeat to make another circle. Wet the paper circle and gently mold around an apple. Use a cotton rag or paper towels to blot and flatten the folds of the paper. Set the apples in a warm place to let the papers dry. Once they dry completely, gently pull the apple out of the paper bowl. Paint the interior of the bowl with a metallic acrylic paint and let dry.

Nest the three bowls inside of your larger bowl to create a pleasing display. Add nuts and dried flowers for an autumn table. (For more on making paper bowls, see page 101.)

## MATERIALS

- colorful, inexpensive papers
- rubber stamps and ink
- embossing powder
- punches
- craft knife
- tissue
- ribbon
- double-sided tape
- shisha mirror appliqués

*Use paper to create festive decorations for any party. For a quick table cover that will invite both laughter and spills, jazz up a roll of brown kraft paper in just a few minutes. Use a paper punch to create windows along each of the long sides, then glue a strip of hot pink tissue to the backside. A row of embossed, rubber stamped designs provides the final border.*

# MEXICAN PAPER PLACE MAT

Kathleen Trenchard

To make a quick and sparkling napkin ring, use double-sided tape to add shisha mirror appliqués to join strip of colorful block-print paper. (When the party's over, use the appliqués for another project since the fusible backing is still intact.)

For a Mexican party, try "papel picado," the Spanish word meaning punched paper. Here, this centuries-old Mexican folk-art technique of papercutting is used to make a sombrero place mat. You'll need one 20" x 14" (51 cm x 36 cm) square sheet of paper per place mat. Use brightly colored "fadeless" paper, butcher paper, simple bond, or brown wrapping paper.

**STEP 1** Fold one sheet of your paper lengthwise. Align the fold edge of the pattern (see page 125) with the fold of the paper, with the pattern on top. To cut multiples, fold all the sheets of paper, align with the pattern and continue as directed below. Use paper clips along all sides to hold papers in place.

**STEP 2** Start at the fold and cut the center crescent shape out. Proceed to cut the larger center shapes by folding on the dotted lines and cutting out the shapes on the fold—there is no need to poke or punch the paper with the scissors. The small holes can be cut this way or can be cut out using a hole punch.

**STEP 3** Finally, cut out the scalloped edge, rearranging your paper clips as needed. When finished, unfold, cover with tissue, and press the folds with an iron. Weave colorful ribbons through the center shapes, attaching underneath with tape. The ties will dangle over the edge of the table. Scroll the name of your guest in the center to make a name card/place mat combination. Now, let the party begin.

*Use sturdy corrugated cardboard to piece together a gift basket that contains fresh baked breads, fruit, spiced olive oil, biscuits, and candles.*

**MATERIALS**

- corrugated cardboard
- colored waxed papers
- tapestry needle
- raffia
- craft knife
- metal ruler
- hole punch
- stapler
- double-sided tape
- gift tags

## DECORATIVE PAPER
# FOOD BASKETS

To make a basket, lay the corrugated board with the ridged side down. Draw a large rectangle, which will be the base of the basket, then draw a 4" (10 cm) lip out from each side of the base. Cut around the exterior of the entire marked shape. Fold each basket side up and punch aligning holes at adjacent edges. Thread a tapestry needle and stitch each corner together with raffia. Cut a strip of corrugated board for the handle and staple it to each long side. Cut stars and add to the base of each handle with double-sided tape.

- Fold and layer pieces of colored wax papers to wrap home-baked breads and pastries.

- For fruit, cut a large square of waxed paper, gather it toward the top, and tie off the pouf with raffia.

- Lay candles in pairs or trios, wrap in two colors of paper, and tie together with raffia.

- Top off mason jars of salsa, jellies, or grains with two colors of waxed paper tied over the lids.

- Make handmade paper labels for homemade oils or jams.

- Shred all your paper scraps to make a bed of grass for the items in your display.

- Crinkle and uncrinkle the waxed paper before you use it to create a different texture.

## VARIATION

Colored waxed papers are also perfect to wrap and present

bouquets of flowers, herbs, or grasses.

*This chapter presents five ideas for using paper in the bedroom, a room that offers peace and respite from the world outside. Here, you will learn a simple technique for creating paper lanterns that can be placed around an electric light source or around candles for an even softer glow. You'll also find a simple pattern for creating a night-light from vellum in dreamy colors of blue and green. The use of punched and pierced patterns in the paper enlivens the design by playing with the light.*

# PAPER BEDROOM

*A simple, unfinished wooden table can be easily transformed into a stylish vanity using printed rayon papers. When adhered to a surface, only the printed pattern remains visible, resulting in an exquisite surface decoration that floats over the underlying paint color.*

*It's the details that complete any room design. A picture frame covered in lizard-skin paper or a tissue-paper painting can add just the finishing touch you need to pull a room together.*

*And as you look for new ways to use paper in your home, remember that it's perfect for decorating a child's room. There's no need to invest in long-term design solutions when children grow and change so much. Decorate the walls by creating colorful star shapes, outdoor scenes or animals from colored, corrugated cardboard. String up a roll of craft paper to the wall behind the bed and have fun drawing new headboard murals on a regular basis. Children will love a room that they can change and interact with.*

- small wood vanity table
- dark plum acrylic paint
- printed rayon paper
- metal ruler
- craft knife
- cutting mat
- acrylic matte medium
- acrylic varnish
- disposable sponge brushes

# LAMINATED-PAPER VANITY TABLE

*Update the charm and delicacy of a lace-topped boudoir table with a much more contemporary material—printed rayon lace papers. Despite their nearly transparent and flimsy appearance, rayon papers are extremely strong and durable. Plain rayon paper is also known as surfboard paper, because after it is printed with an image or design, the paper is laid into a surfboard or skateboard and covered with resin. The paper virtually disappears, leaving only the printed design. The paper used here is printed with delicate white wavy lines. Though the printed paper is absolutely beautiful on its own, it stands out even more when applied to a darker surface; the paper's background becomes ghosted, leaving the delicate white lines floating over the surface.*

# LAMINATED-PAPER VANITY TABLE

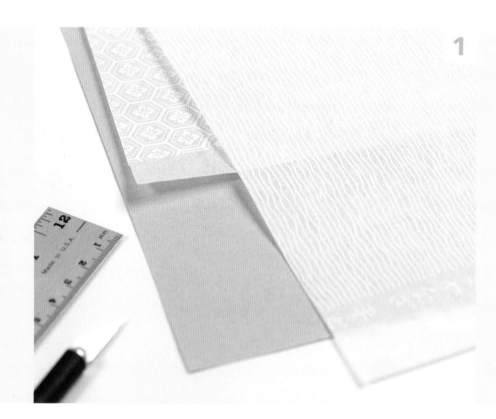

**STEP 1** For a table that has been previously painted or varnished, clean thoroughly with soap and water and a cloth or scrub brush. Sand the surface with a coarse grade of sandpaper, then wipe with a damp cloth to remove any dust. Paint it in your color of choice using a sponge brush to apply two even coats of acrylic paint. For a new wood table, seal any holes or cracks with wood filler. Then sand the surface with medium-grade sandpaper. Add one coat of acrylic wood primer and two coats of acrylic paint. Test-fit the pieces of paper on your table. Measure the top surface of the table and any drawers or apron panels where you would like to place the paper. Using a metal ruler, craft knife, and cutting mat, carefully measure and cut a piece of rayon paper for each section.

## VARIATION

Experiment with different styles of printed rayon paper over a stained natural wood finish to create an entryway table. Here, a Japanese geometric-patterned paper was applied to a table that was not painted, but rather, colored with a dark acrylic stain. Add a detail at the bottom of each leg by wrapping it with a 1" (3 cm) strip of the same paper (as seen on page 65).

**STEP 2** Working only one section at a time, lay the paper in place. If you are planning to cover more than one section of your table, start with a small section first to get used to the process. To work on an apron or a drawer, place the furniture in such a way that you are always working parallel to the floor. With the paper in place, use a sponge brush and acrylic medium to laminate the paper to the surface of the table. Start from the center of the paper and work out to the edges. Because the paper is so strong and the acrylic medium not that sticky, you can pull up and reposition the paper as needed to make sure you have a perfect fit. Smooth the sponge brush repeatedly along the entire surface, always working toward the edges to remove all air bubbles. Be sure that the entire surface of the paper is evenly soaked with acrylic medium to ensure an even, translucent effect. Let each section dry completely before you paper another one. Once the acrylic medium is completely dry, give your papered surface at least two coats of satin acrylic varnish to finish and protect it.

- 12" x 16" (30 cm x 41 cm) sturdy translucent paper for shade

- small sheet of translucent paper for triangle accents

- stiff paper to use as a pattern

- scissors

- craft knife

- cutting mat

- PVA glue

- cotton swab or narrow paintbrush

- bone folder

- pillar candle

# JAPANESE GLOW LANTERNS

*Simple geometric shapes add a little play to these easy-to-make paper lamps. Choose two papers that will diffuse the light differently. That subtle contrast will make your lamp more interesting. Use a sturdy medium-weight paper for the shade, one that has enough body to stand firmly on its own. For the triangle accents, you can use a lighter weight paper since the firmer base paper will support it. The construction is simple—the paper is merely notched along the overlapping edges and folded over. The notches hold the cylinder together firmly while adding a decorative cut that releases pure light.*

**STEP 1**  Prepare your papers. Cut a 12" x 16" (30 cm x 41 cm) piece of sturdy paper; this will be your shade. Cut several triangles from the accent paper. It's best to make a pattern and use that to keep your triangles uniform in size. Once the triangles are cut, trim 3/8" (9.5 cm) off each edge of your pattern, and use the remaining smaller triangle to mark and cut triangles from your shade paper.

**STEP 2**  With the front of your shade paper facing down, fold a 1/2" (1 cm) hem in the top and bottom long edges. Next, use a cotton swab or a narrow paintbrush to spread a thin line of glue around one of the cut triangles on the shade. Lay a paper triangle, front side down, behind the cutout. Press the edges of the paper together to adhere. Repeat to cover each of the cut holes with a paper triangle.

To further enhance a crumpled paper, immerse the ball into a diluted tea bath. The softened fibers at the folds will absorb the dye more easily than the rest of the sheet and enhance the crumpled effect.

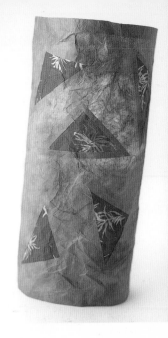

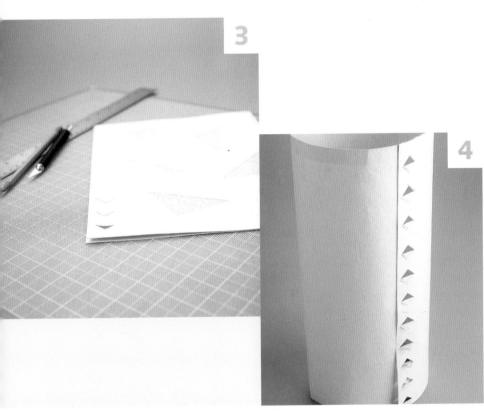

## JAPANESE GLOW LANTERNS

### VARIATION

Before you start your project, crumple the paper for your glow lamp to give it extra texture. The folds will weaken the paper, allowing more light to shine through those areas. Fold and unfold the paper gently so it doesn't tear, and allow the paper to flatten again after unfolding by weighting it under heavy books or by ironing it using a pressing cloth.

**STEP 3** With the paper still lying flat, lift the left (short) edge and fold it over to align with the right edge. Using care not to crush the curved side of the paper, carefully mark and cut five $1/2$" (1 cm) upside down V shapes through both layers of paper and evenly spaced along the short side of the papers.

**STEP 4** Open the paper and reroll into a cylinder shape with the upside down V shapes aligned again. Push the cut V from the inside of the shade, folding out and down so that the papers interlock. Glue the V tabs in place to secure your glow lamp's cylindrical shape.

- artist canvas

- tissue papers in assorted colors: 3 shades of blue, 2 shades each of green and lavender

- animal or other printed tissue-paper

- acrylic matte medium

- acrylic varnish

- scissors

- soft paintbrush

# TISSUE-PAPER PAINTING

*Need to brighten up a small corner? Create a simple tissue-paper collage on a pre-made canvas. Any craft or gift tissue works perfectly, and you can even introduce patterned papers to add a little flair. Here, a simple trio of tulips sprouts from an impressionistic background. By working with several shades of colored tissue, as you see here in the sky and the grass areas, it's easy to add gradations that fade from light to dark.*

# TISSUE-PAPER PAINTING

**STEP 1** Prepare your papers. Tear the green and blue tissue into approximate 1" to 1 1/2" (3 cm to 4 cm) pieces. Keep piles of each color separated.

**STEP 2** Start to adhere the tissue to the canvas, alternating shades of blue tissue for the sky. To apply a piece of tissue, lay it on the canvas in the desired position, then use a brush dipped in acrylic matte medium to wet the tissue and paint it onto the surface. Smooth out the paper entirely by gently brushing out any wrinkles with the tip of the brush. Overlap subsequent pieces to achieve full coverage. Use alternating pieces of the two lightest shades of blue at the top of the painting, slowly integrating pieces of the deepest blue as you move toward the horizon line. After you work halfway down the sky area, stop using the lightest shade and use only the two darker ones.

**STEP 3** Continue filling in the background of the painting, being sure to completely cover the sides of the canvas. Use two shades of green for the grass. After some of the grass is filled in under the horizon line, lay the flower stems down. To create a flower stem, tear a long narrow piece of printed tissue. You can test fit the length by holding it over the canvas. Once they are in place, cover the bottom of each stem slightly with the green tissue so it looks as if it is emerging from the grass.

**STEP 4** Cut three tulip shapes freehand. Adhere them to the top of the stem. Let the tissue painting dry completely. Add two coats of an acrylic varnish to protect the painting, drying thoroughly between each coat.

## TISSUE-PAPER PAINTING

### VARIATION

To add more complexity to a tissue collage, add several layers of tissue. In this example, tissue paper in pink, orange, red, and maroon were overlaid in torn horizontal strips. The colors blend and merge, creating a nice secondary palette. Here, one graphic flower shape in orange is used to complete the design. Experiment by adding pieces of other fun scraps such as newspapers, gift wrap, handwritten notes, and cancelled stamps into your collage paintings. Or, for a dramatic effect, create a series of three themed collages to hang together.

## MATERIALS

- 1 unfinished frame

- 1 sheet lizard or other
  decorative textured paper

- acrylic paint

- paintbrush

- decoupage medium
  or PVA glue

- craft knife

- cutting mat

- pencil

- metal ruler

- sandpaper

# LIZARD-SKIN FRAME

*A small piece of special paper goes a long way when it's used to dress a picture frame. The frame featured here uses an exquisite paper that resembles lizard skin. The surface of this paper is laminated so it doesn't require any type of varnish to protect it. You can start with an unfinished wood frame as we did, or give any existing frame a new look—just sand the surface lightly and add a coat of primer before you start your project. For a very finished look, choose a paper with body and an interesting texture reminiscent of leather or animal skin.*

# LIZARD-SKIN FRAME

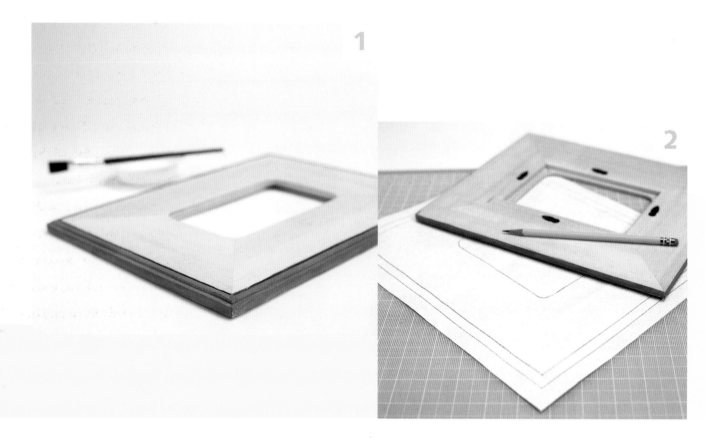

**STEP 1** Sand the unfinished frame to smooth out any imperfections and remove any remaining dust with a damp cloth. Using acrylic paint, coat the side edges with paint, extending the paint over the front face of your frame by 1/2" (1 cm). Paint the inner lip of the frame and let dry. Add a second coat.

**STEP 2** Lay the decorative paper face down on your work surface. Remove the backing and glass from the frame and lay face down over the paper. Trace the exterior and interior borders of the frame with a pencil. Measure in 3/8" (1 cm) from outer traced line to indicate the adjusted cutting line. Using a craft knife, ruler, and cutting mat, cut out the frame shape at the adjusted border. Then, carefully cut out the center hole.

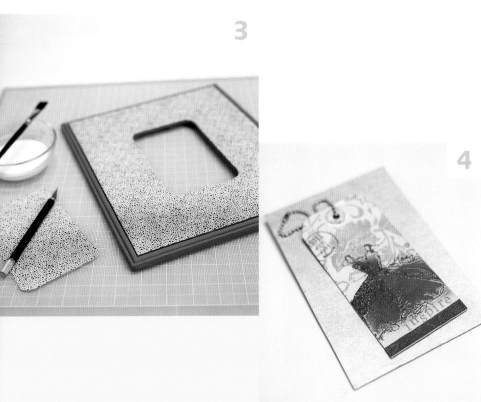

### VARIATION

To cover a frame entirely with paper, trace the exterior as in the previous project, then measure and draw a second border around it equal to the depth of the frame. Extend the lines of the frame's actual border out to the second border—you will now have a square marked at each corner. Trim out the corner squares and glue the paper to the frame, smoothing the paper out and around each edge.

**STEP 3** Apply decoupage medium or glue to the back of the paper and carefully center it on the front face of the frame. Gently smooth the paper from the center, working outward to eliminate any air bubbles and ensure good adhesion.

**STEP 4** The stamped collages made by Dawn Houser, are created on manila shipping tags using Dawn's Daydreams collection of rubber stamps. (See Resources list for more information.) To create beautiful collages like this, layer stamped and cut images over a printed pattern created with background stamps. Embellish your designs using embossing powders, metallic inks, and colored paper accents. You will have memorable art worthy of your stylish frame.

## MATERIALS

- two 8 ½" x 11" (22 cm x 28 cm) sheets of turquoise and olive green vellum

- flower-shaped paper punch

- sturdy cardboard or mat board

- scissors

- white acrylic paint

- craft knife

- metal ruler

- pencil

- PVA glue

# PIN-PRICKED VELLUM
# NIGHT-LIGHT SHADES

*This glowing night-light is made from punched and layered vellum. Vellum, once a difficult commodity to find, is now widely available in a huge array of colors and patterns. Real vellum is actually the skin of a goat or calf, but much of what is seen in stores these days is a version made from vegetable fibers. Vellum is the perfect weight and translucency for making quick and pretty night-lights—it's also very sturdy. This project features a deep turquoise blue and an olive green color scheme for a cool, sleep-inducing color combination. Here, the vellum is curved around and attached to a cardboard backing that slides over any simple night-light fixture. You can trim the back plate of your design to work with any specific fixture as needed.*

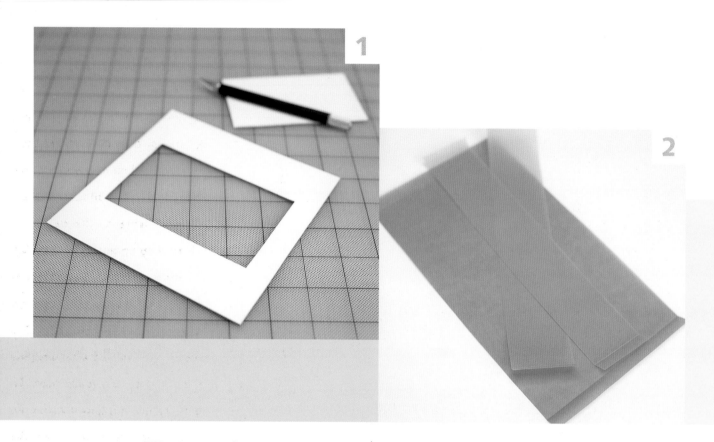

**STEP 1** Measure and cut a 6" x 6" (15 cm x 15 cm) square of sturdy cardboard. Cut a switch-plate-sized hole (2 ³/₄" x 4 ¹/₂" [7 cm x 11 cm]) into the center. Paint the front side with two coats of white acrylic paint.

**STEP 2** Measure and cut a 6" x 11" (15 cm x 28 cm) piece from the turquoise sheet of vellum. Lay the sheet out on a flat surface. Create a ¹/₂" (1 cm) fold along each short side, with both folds made toward the front (top) of the paper. Cut two 2" x 11" (5 cm x 28 cm) strips of olive vellum and make a similar ¹/₂" (1 cm) fold on each short end of these strips, also folding toward the top.

**STEP 3** Punch five flowers, space evenly along the two long sides of the turquoise sheet but within the area between the two folds. Lay the sheet on your work surface with the folds facing up. Lay an olive-colored strip along the top and bottom of the turquoise sheet to back each flowered border. Nest the folds of the olive sheet with the turquoise sheet. Thin a small amount of PVA glue with 25 percent water, and then paint it into the folds to secure the sheets together. Let dry.

**STEP 4** Bend the completed vellum shade into a half cylinder shape and fit the back plate into the folded edges with the painted side facing the vellum. Adhere the folds to the rear edges of the back plate using PVA glue.

PIN-PRICKED VELLUM NIGHT-LIGHT SHADES

## VARIATION

Use a sturdy embroidery needle or any sharp tool to add pinpricked patterns to the shade. The perforations will add an interesting texture to the surface and add a dotted line of backlighting to the shade. To create a pinpricked design, lay the paper over a yielding surface, such as a small stack of newspapers. Here, the pinpricks were designed to resemble the path of a bee stopping at the flowers along his path. To re-create this design, use a craft knife to cut the bee shape from the turquoise vellum at the same time you punch the flowers. Then create the bee's looping path. (See page 126 for bee pattern.)

*When treated the right way, paper can even be used in the bath. I
have always loved the ingenious bath that my mother-in-law designed
using* New Yorker *magazine covers as wallpaper—the colorful
illustrations never fail to delight. The projects presented here are in
the same spirit. They use simple materials that create surprising
and fun results.*

# PAPER BATH

*The humble materials and techniques of papier-mâché make a real
statement when they are used to construct a mirrored cosmetic
cabinet. Top this cabinet off with a painted finish and guests will
wonder where you found such a little treasure. You'll also find out
how to use scraps of tissue paper with copper leaf flakes to create
laminated bath jars that resemble the smoky colors and the metallic
sparkle of ancient Roman glass. Use your jars to display bath salts,
lotions, and perfumes. Or, for a boutique look, capture a collage of
all your favorite things within plastic laminating sheets and use them
to construct a playful wastebasket. All these projects will live happily
in a dewy environment and look great for years to come.*

## MATERIALS

- 1 sheet mat board
- newspapers torn into 1"(3 cm) strips
- white glue
- paintbrush
- paper tape
- acrylic paint
- craft knife
- metal ruler
- cutting mat
- linen bookbinding tape
- 4 $\frac{1}{2}$" x 4 $\frac{1}{2}$"(11 cm x 11 cm) beveled mirror
- acrylic varnish

# PAPER-STRIP LIPSTICK CABINET

It's easy to use a framework of cardboard covered with strips of paper to construct a small, mirrored cabinet. The craft of creating objects from layers of pasted paper has been around ever since waste paper has been available. This simple building technique allows a lot of flexibility in design—virtually any shape can be achieved, and the resulting sculptural pieces are lightweight and durable. Here, the base of the cabinet is cut from a flat sheet of cardboard that is folded up and around at the bottom to create the shelf. The shelf is then stabilized with the wrapped strips of paper. The mirror is taped to the back using a strong linen bookbinding tape.

# PAPER-STRIP LIPSTICK CABINET

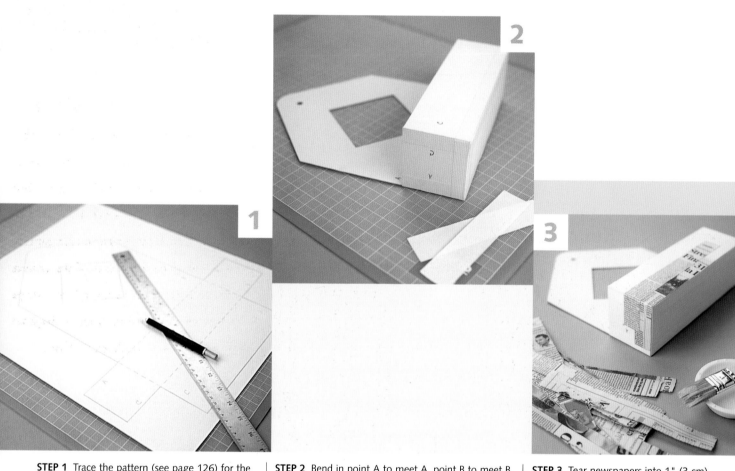

**STEP 1** Trace the pattern (see page 126) for the cabinet onto the mat board. Using a craft knife, metal ruler, and cutting mat, cut out the pattern from the mat board. Score dashed lines. Turn the board over.

**STEP 2** Bend in point A to meet A, point B to meet B, and so forth, to make sure the edges of the shelf align. Adjust as needed. Secure the shelf edges with paper tape.

**STEP 3** Tear newspapers into 1" (3 cm) strips. Pour white glue into disposable container and dilute by 10 percent. Using a paintbrush, apply the glue to a strip of newspaper and apply the strip to the cabinet; start by covering all adjoining edges, and apply the strips horizontally. Be sure to overlap edges of the strips as you go, and start and end the strips in a staggered fashion. Continue until the entire cabinet, front and back, has been covered with at least three layers of strips. Let dry completely for one to seven days, depending on the temperature.

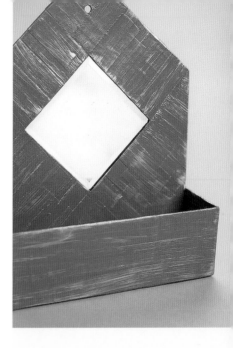

Experiment with the texture and finish of your paper to make it resemble wood, stone, clay, or even metal. For example, you can add sand to your paint for a sandstone finish, paint a faux wood grain using feathers and umber washes, or add a thick layer of molding paste to give the impression of clay.

## VARIATION

PAPER-STRIP LIPSTICK CABINET

The paper strips and the finishes that are applied to them can create unique surface designs. Even just applying your strips in a specific direction can create a nice pattern. Here, the back plate of the cabinet was wrapped with all the strips moving outward from a diagonal center to look like rays of sun.

**STEP 4** Paint the entire cabinet with two coats of a solid color, allowing it to dry between coats. Then, using a barely damp sponge, gently give a rubbed coating of silver paint over the top, moving the sponge in the same direction as the strips of paper, leaving much of the base color still exposed. Let dry. Seal with two coats of acrylic varnish.

**STEP 5** Place the mirror behind the opening and attach using linen bookbinding tape.

## MATERIALS

- glass bottles with stoppers
- colored tissue paper
- water-based varnish
- metallic reflecting medium or interference paint
- soft-bristled, round paintbrush
- copper or silver leaf
- oil-based copper or silver leafing cream
- scissors

# PAPER-FROSTED BATH JARS

*Tissue paper laminated onto glass makes a magical combination in this fun project. The cloudy tissue paper, soaked with varnish and washed with a reflecting medium and the flakes of leaf, makes these bottles resemble ancient glass from the Roman Empire, the era when glassblowing was invented. When wet with varnish, the tissue paper seems to practically melt onto the glass, creating this unique effect. The wrinkles that appear as the tissue conforms to the glass only add to the character of these decorative pieces.*

# PAPER-FROSTED BATH JARS

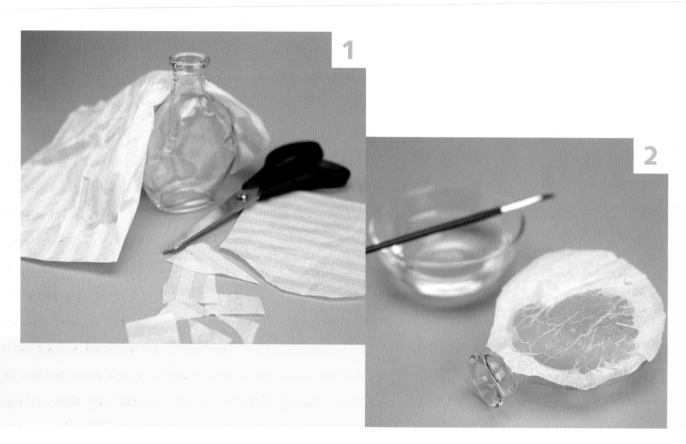

**STEP 1** Cut out a tissue piece large enough to comfortably wrap around the bottle. Cut a few extra small pieces for filling in any bare spots later on. Clean the surface of the bottle with alcohol or glass cleaner to remove any oils.

**STEP 2** Lay the tissue against one face of glass. Dip a soft brush into the water-based varnish. Start painting the tissue onto the surface working from the center of the bottle outward. Keep the brush fairly wet with varnish as you work around the bottle. When you get to curves in the bottle where the tissue will overlap considerably, trim away pieces of excess tissue. Continue painting and molding the tissue to the glass. Add small pieces of tissue to fill in around the neck or any bare areas. Mix a few drops of metallic or iridescent paint with a few drops of varnish. Lightly brush this mixture over your entire bottle.

**STEP 3** Tear up leafing paper in small pieces. Use your clean brush to wet small areas at a time with varnish, then apply small flecks of leaf to the surface, painting over each piece with varnish to adhere. Apply the flecks in diagonal swirls and patches over the bottle.

**STEP 4** Rub an oil-based metallic leafing cream around the lip of the bottle for the finishing touch. Let your bottle dry completely. Use your jars for bath salts and bath oils.

## VARIATION

Use this same technique to decorate other glass objects. Here, a piece of Chinese joss paper was used to create a modern design on this flower vase. Joss paper is a light tissue paper that comes with a square of leaf attached to the center. To ensure the tissue behind the leafed area adheres well to the glass, paint some varnish on the glass first. Then lay down the joss paper and continue to smooth it against the glass from the top with more varnish. In Chinese culture, joss paper is traditionally burned as a way of sending goodwill to a departed spirit. For another project that uses joss paper, see page 115 in the Gallery section. To make your own joss paper, apply a square of gold or silver leaf to a lightweight tissue paper using diluted PVA glue.

## MATERIALS

- laminating machine or clear laminating film
- paper scraps for collage: magazine pages, postcards, wallpaper, decoupage scraps, color photocopies
- printed paper (visible on basket interior)
- 1/8" (8 mm) hole punch
- scissors
- waxed cotton cord
- silver beads
- tapestry needle
- artist's tape (optional)

# LAMINATED COLLAGE WASTEBASKET

*Who says bathrooms can't be fun? Laminate a collection of your favorite images to create a stylish wastebasket. The four sides and the bottom of the basket are punched with holes and sewn together with a simple whipstitch. To unify the basket, each side of the collage is backed with a common printed paper, in this case a leopard print, so that the insides of the basket match. You can embellish your finished basket with beads, buttons, or colorful ribbon to add a personal touch.*

*There are several options for laminating. You can purchase laminating paper in rolls and laminate the papers yourself. There are also laminating machines available for home use, which you may want to invest in if you plan to do lots of laminating. In addition, many full-service copy facilities have professional laminating machines available for customer use. All of the aforementioned methods are suitable for this project.*

# LAMINATED COLLAGE WASTEBASKET

**STEP 1** Cut out papers to use for your collage. Find large pieces that will work well as background papers, then look for interesting images for the foreground. Try to find multiple images with similar themes so that you work related images around all the sides. The featured basket combines images from art, garden and decorating magazines, air balloons from a wallpaper border, photocopied images of various musicians, and scraps from Japanese comic strips.

**STEP 2** Determine the size of the four sides of your basket. Cut out four rectangles of the printed paper 1" (3 cm) smaller, in each dimension, than the desired size of your basket. Cut one additional square of printed paper equal to the width of the rectangular sides. (This will be the bottom of the basket.) Lay the printed sheet with the front side facing down, and arrange your collage on top (facing up) so the edges of the collage are aligned with the edges of the printed paper. If you are using a laminating machine, assemble the papers right on the laminating tray. When everything is in position, feed the assemblage through. Otherwise, put one sheet of laminating film on your work surface adhesive side up and tape it in place with artist's tape. Lay the printed paper down as explained above, put the collage in place on top, and apply the final layer of laminating film over the entire assemblage. Continue to laminate the other three sides of the basket. Laminate only the printed sheet for the bottom of the basket. Trim and square all the sides around the collage to the predetermined size. You should have approximately 1/2" (1 cm) inch of pure film around all sides of the collage.

To use your caddy for smaller items, consider sewing the edges of the pockets with your sewing machine, then just use the perle cotton whipstitches to secure the pockets together and hold them to the frame. (Use a denim-weight sewing machine needle and strong thread.)

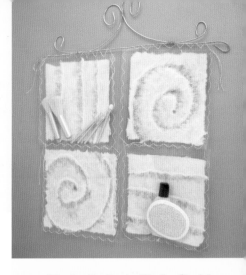

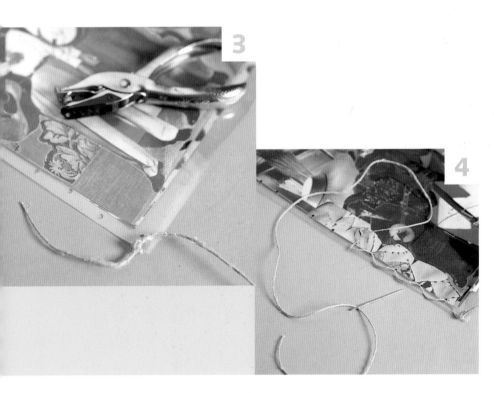

**STEP 3** Starting ½" (1 cm) in from the edge, punch holes, each 1" (3 cm) apart along each long side and the bottom of each rectangle. To have perfectly matched sides, lay two adjacent printed sides together and punch them at the same time.

**STEP 4** Thread a tapestry needle with waxed cotton cord. Begin by securing two sides together through the bottom set of matching punched holes. Tie the ends of cord securely, then continue sewing the two sides together with a whipstitch. To make a whipstitch, start from the back and pull the thread up through the two layers. Wrap the cord around the layers. Again insert the needle from the bottom of the next set of holes. Continue in this fashion and then knot the cord in the last set of holes. Leave an extra few inches of cording for tying on beads. Continue stitching all the sides together. Then stitch the bottom piece in the same fashion, with the printed side facing in. String beads onto the extra cording and tie an overhand knot below them to secure.

## LAMINATED COLLAGE WASTEBASKET

### V A R I A T I O N

Make a laminated bath caddy by sewing together four plastic pockets and securing them to an armature frame. Make the back panel of the pocket by cutting a 7" x 7" (18 cm x 18 cm) piece of decorative paper and laminating it. Trim out the laminated piece, leaving ½" (1 cm) of pure film surrounding the paper. Repeat to make four panels. Next, cut four 8" x 8" (20 cm x 20 cm) pieces of overhead film (available from stationery stores) to make the front panels. Cut an extra ½" (1 cm) off the top edge of each front panel. Pair up the front and back panels. Punch holes 1" (3 cm) apart around all sides of each set. Note: On the top edge, the holes will only be punched in the back panel. Using silver perle cotton or similar weight thread, whipstitch the bottom three sides of the pockets together. Then, stitch the top of the bottom squares to the bottom of the top squares. Use 10-gauge aluminum-covered copper wire to create a frame. Using the picture for reference, bend each of the pieces and wire them together with a 20-gauge silver-colored wire. Then stitch the tops of the top squares to the wire frame.

# PAPER CRAFTS GALLERY

*This Paper Crafts Gallery section presents a selection of twenty other paper art objects that can be used in and around the home. Many of the artists who contributed are specialists devoted to the art of hand papermaking. Others are designers who work in several mediums but who also enjoy experimenting with paper art. The pieces in this collection range from simple pinwheels and paper frames to elaborate lamps and wall hangings constructed from unique handmade papers also made by the artists. Some of the more elaborate pieces also offer simpler alternatives for construction in additon to the methods employed by the artists. This is just a small sampling of the many options for using paper to decorate your home. Let it be a starting point for you to begin creating on your own with this simple and beautiful medium. See the Artist Resource page for additional information on Gallery contributors.*

## MATERIALS

- two 13" (33 cm) squares of ivory handmade paper

- black walnut hull dye

- india ink

- Japanese brush

- embroidery floss

- paper clips

- poly-fill

- wheat, or konnyaku, flour (optional)

*This delicate pillow makes the perfect accent. Create a pattern of repetitive squares using a black walnut hull dye and india ink applied with a Japanese brush, or rubber stamping with a waterproof ink. The pillow is constructed with handmade paper made from long abaca fibers.*

# MEDITATION PILLOW

*Winnie Radolan*

**STEP 1** Make or cut to size two 13" (33 cm) squares of handmade paper. Using a soft Japanese paintbrush, create an all-over pattern using dye and inks, or a rubber-stamp. Let the designs dry.

**STEP 2** Crinkle the paper into a ball several times. Before starting this step, to help hold the wrinkles and make the paper flexible and supple, you may wish to coat one side of each pillow square with wheat (konnyaku) flour, prepared according to package directions. (The artist coated the backside of the patterned piece so as not to risk having the dye run.) Allow the paper to sit for about fifteen minutes, and then wrinkle and crinkle it into a ball. Stretch the paper back out to let it completely dry.

**STEP 3** Line up front and back pillow pieces and fasten them together with large paperclips. To complete the knife-edged pillow, hand stitch the sections together with decorative top stitching using six-strand embroidery floss in a matching color. If you have a zigzag sewing machine, try an open top stitch to attach the pillow sides together. Leave an opening just large enough to add poly-fill stuffing. Fluff it out and insert it into your pillow evenly, being careful to fill corners. Complete the topstitching.

*This bowl was created by using the sheet forming technique of dipping the mold into a vat of cotton paper pulp. The pulp was then transferred to a mold in several layers to build thickness. The lip around the bowl was made by allowing the pulp to extend around the edge of the bowl that was used as the mold. The finished bowl was brushed with pearlescent pigments added to paint and acrylic medium.*

## MATERIALS

- ready-to-use cotton paper pulp

- blender, if using cotton linters

- vat

- bowl to use as a mold

- release agent such as silicon or liquid wax

- screen wire mesh

- wool blanket or Pellon

- sponge

- pearlescent pigment added to acrylic paints and gel medium

- paintbrush

# PAPER BOWL

**STEP 1** Coat an existing bowl with a release agent such as silicon or liquid wax. Place the bowl upside down on a piece of non-cotton fabric–a wool blanket or Pellon from a fabric store works well.

**STEP 2** Using a piece of screen wire mesh held taut, dip into a vat of pulp to catch an even layer of fibers. Let this drain for a few seconds before inverting it onto the surface of the bowl. With a sponge, press the back of the screen to release the surface tension and transfer the pulp to the bowl. Continue until the bowl surface is completely covered to thickness desired. To create a flat lip around the bowl, simply place the pulp at the edge of the bowl and let it extend out onto the blanket. When the application of pulp is complete, place the wire screen on top of the pulp and press with the sponge. Repeatedly press around the entire surface. Pressing removes extra water and produces a more solid finished product.

**STEP 3** Let the bowl dry. The drying is by evaporation, so heat, humidity, and airflow are the determining factors of drying time. When dry, the bowl will pop off the mould and be ready for any embellishments.

**STEP 4** Paint the bowl on the inside using pearlescent pigments mixed into paint or gel medium. These pigments give a subtle shimmer and shine to the surface.

*Fran Lacy*

## MATERIALS

- willow, grapevine, or other found straight and flexible tree/bush branches
- raffia
- waxed linen
- Japanese paper—make your own or purchase papers such as kozo, washi, or unryu
- methylcellulose or PVA glue
- socket—keyless, standard base
- 2 locknuts
- 4" (10 cm) cross bar (fixture strap)
- 1 1/2" (4 cm) to 2" (5 cm) threaded nipple (lamp pipe)
- 8' (2.4 m) cord set with plug
- cord switch
- 40-watt bulb

*This beautiful illuminated sculpture is made from willow branches and handmade paper. The willow is peeled and then soaked until it becomes pliable enough to work into a fluid armature that is secured with threads and raffia. Once the armature is completed, damp sheets of paper are applied to each area of the armature grid, creating a subtle patchwork of colors.*

# SKIN & BONES LAMP

**STEP 1** Gather twelve straight willow shoots, or other similar straight and flexible branch, vine or reed. Each piece should measure 18" to 24" (46 cm x 61) in length. You can also purchase basket reed and vine.

**STEP 2** Scrape off the outer bark of the harvested willow. Then soak the willow or basket reed in water for about an hour.

**STEP 3** To begin the armature, bundle six willow shoots. Tie the tips together with waxed linen about 4" (10 cm) from the tip and then wrap over the waxed linen with raffia. Loosely wrap the bottom willow ends together with masking tape. Cut off any uneven ends.

**STEP 4** Make five willow or grape vine rings increasing in diameter from 3" to 6" (8 cm x 15 cm). Overlap the ends of the rings, then tie and wrap with waxed lined and raffia.

**STEP 5** Insert the first ring a bit below the raffia-wrapped tip and tie each willow shoot to the ring, first with waxed linen, then wrap with raffia. You may need to hold the ring in place with clamps or masking tape.

**STEP 6** Next, attach a 4" (10 cm) ring for the base, and to hold the electrical works. Remove the masking tape from the base. Insert the ring about 2" to 3" (5 cm x 8 cm) from the bottom, and tie and wrap as above. Insert and secure three additional rings into the armature as pictured.

**STEP 7** Install the lighting element. Begin by screwing the threaded 1 1/2" (4 cm) lamp pipe (nipple) into the lamp socket base. Next, screw the 4" (10 cm) cross bar (or fixture strap) into the pipe below the socket and tighten both ends with a lock nut. Follow the wiring instructions on the lamp socket package.

**STEP 8** Place the lighting hardware on the top-side of the base ring. Secure with waxed linen and wrap with raffia. The socket should be in the center of the armature. It is important that the socket be centered so the light bulb does not come in contact with the paper skin. Following the package directions, attach the cord switch to the cord.

**STEP 9** Cover the armature with paper. Make your own paper or purchase Japanese papers such as kozo, washi, or unryu papers. The paper can be dampened, then torn or cut to match the armature area to be covered. Stretch the paper taut over the willow and gently press the paper edges together. The wet paper fibers will bond to each other. Brush on a solution of methylcellulose to reinforce each seam, or use a solution of diluted PVA glue.

**STEP 10** As the paper dries, it will shrink around the armature. Use a hair dryer to speed up the drying process; you will have better control and can smooth out any unwanted wrinkles in the paper.

## TIP

The paper does not require any kind of fire retardant as long as the bulb does not touch the paper. Use a 40-watt, or less, bulb and provide a heat release for the bulb. This can be accomplished by piercing a few holes in the paper near the heat source and near the top. Another option is to not cover an area within the armature.

*Linda Louise Horn*

## MATERIALS

- basketball, soccer ball, or a Pyrex bowl to use as a mold
- 8–10 sheets of paper in each of four colors (featured here: dark and light green, peach and cream)
- 1" (2.5 cm) flat brush for gluing
- package of copper leaf foil
- scissors
- deckle-edge scissors
- PVA glue
- masking tape
- petroleum jelly or silicone spray
- jar or tin can large enough to rest your mold on
- matte varnish

*Elizabeth Kosterich*

## TIPS

- Allow yourself several days to complete this project. Let it dry thoroughly between layers for the best results. If you do more than one layer at a time, you risk it not drying well and mildew may set in!

- It is much easier to cut the copper foil if you leave it in between the tissue paper sheets it comes with and cut through the tissue.

*In this project, the full roundness of a layered-paper bowl is accentuated by using a combination of triangles that actually point to the curves. Although the bowl uses soft colors and appears fragile, the multiple layers of paper create a piece of substantial strength. This bowl should not used be with any liquids, but as a decorative sculpture it will take quite a lot of handling and use.*

# BRONZE TRIANGLE BOWL

**Day One** Set up a mold using a basketball with the midpoint taped off. Tape the fully inflated ball to a jar or tin can so that it is high enough to work on easily. Lightly coat the ball with petroleum jelly or spray of silicone. Layer with wet squares and triangles of paper, no larger than three inches (6 cm). Overlap as you go. Let the wet paper adhere to itself—pattern is not important. This inner layer will not be seen. Use this and the next two or three layers to practice. Let the top edges that overhang be uneven. Dry thoroughly overnight.

**Day Two** Apply another layer to the bowl, only this time coat the dry paper on both sides with the PVA glue. Again, practice your pattern and techniques on this layer as it will not show. Let this layer dry overnight.

**Days Three and Four** Create a third layer, as above, and using PVA glue to adhere the pieces.

**Day Five** This is the final outside layer—it will be visible. Divide the mold area into eight sections by placing masking tape on the lower, unused sections of your mold. Using dark green, cut four tall, narrow triangles and glue as pictured. Make the triangles slightly larger than the 1/8th tape marker, and fit one into every other space. Cut four slightly smaller triangles in peach and lay them in the opposite direction. Use deckle-edge scissors for a softer torn effect. Glue peach triangles in the spaces between the green triangles, making sure to cover the edges of the green triangles with the peach. Let dry overnight.

**Day Six** Cut small triangles of light green and apply within peach triangles. Alternate with cream if you wish. Finish with a layer of small triangles cut from copper foil. Be patient gluing the foil as it tears very easily. Try appling glue to the bowl and laying the foil on top. Burnish lightly with a dry brush. Let dry overnight.

**Day Seven** Gently remove the bowl from the mold, invert it, and place it on a flat surface. You may find that deflating the ball helps to accomplish this more easily. Gently tear up small (about 1" [3 cm]) uneven squares/bits of all the paper colors. Working from the bottom center of the inside, glue the entire interior in a patchwork pattern. Let dry overnight.

**Day Eight** Spray bowl, inside and out, with a matte varnish for protection against dirt and to ensure the copper foil doesn't tarnish.

*This lively sun wall plaque is created from papier-mâché formed in a plaster mold. The shape is first modeled in clay, then a plaster cast is poured to make a mold for the pulp. In the studio of the PaperSun Paper Makers, on the island of Syros, Greece, the sun is an important motif. They chose the sun as a symbol for the creativity and the joy of making paper art.*

# PAPER SUN

**STEP 1** Nail four strips of wood to the edges of the wood square to make a frame. Shape a sun out of modeling clay. Press designs into the clay using modeling and embossing tools. Set the clay face up within the frame and coat it with linseed oil. Prepare the plaster and pour it over the sun to make a casting. Let the casting dry completely. Remove the clay sun to reveal the plaster mold.

**STEP 2** Tear the cardboard into pieces (approximately 1" x 1" [3 cm x 3 cm]) and boil in water for about thirty minutes. Then leave it to soak overnight. Turn it into papier-mâché pulp with a blender. Put the pulp into a piece of cheesecloth and wring out the water. Add glue, sawdust, and lime to the pulp and knead together thoroughly.

**STEP 3** Press the paper mâché into the mold, filling the mold. Drying may take from two days to two weeks. Take care that your star sun remains flat by putting weight on those parts that are already dry. When completely dry, remove the sun from the mold.

**STEP 4** Paint the dry sun with tempera paint. Add a hanger to the back to complete your colorful wall decoration. The mold can be used and again. Consider making a set of three to hang over an entryway.

## MATERIALS

*For the star sun:*

- For approximately 10 ounces (300 g) papier-mâché:
- 8 ounces (250 g) cardboard
- 1 ounce (30 g) sawdust
  ½ teaspoon lime
- 1 ⅓ teaspoons wood glue
- blender or Hollander beater
- a plastic board, about 10" x 10" (25 cm x 25 cm)
- permanent marker
- linseed oil
- clay-modeling tools
- different objects with interesting shapes for embossing
- brushes for tempera
- tempera paint
- cheesecloth

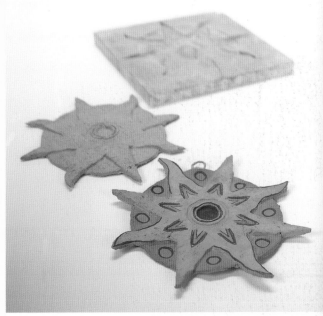

*Monika Dimitrakopoulos-Lang*

*For the mold:*

- modeling clay
- plaster
- 10" (25 cm) square piece of wood
- 4 pieces of wood to fit the edges for a frame
- hammer
- nails

## MATERIALS

- cooking pan
- wooden stir stick
- blender or Hollander beater
- 3 plastic bowls
- square sheet of Plexiglas (in the size you would like your mirror frame to be; the featured mirror is 10"x 10" [25 cm x 25 cm])
- permanent marker
- ceramic modeling tools
- sponge
- piece of cotton fabric
- leather thread
- brushes
- cardboard (Asian)
- white and blue copy paper
- mirror
- natural pigments (ocher)
- ultramarine
- wallpaper paste
- white glue
- acrylic varnish or shellac
- 4" (10 cm) twisted paper thread
- linen bookbinding tape

*This mirror is part of a series of mirrors created while the artist was exploring different possibilities and techniques with papier-mâché. The design is inspired by a classical Greek figure, but with modern eyes.*

# MIRROR FRAME

**STEP 1** Tear the cardboard in 1" (3 cm) pieces, the white and blue copy paper into ½" pieces. Keep all the pieces separate. Boil each of the three separately for half an hour and let sit overnight. Use a blender to turn each into a pulp. Divide the pulp in half. In one half, add two to three teaspoons of ocher pigment and glue to make a dark yellow. Combine the other half with the white paper pulp and a little more glue to make a light yellow. Add ultramarine pigment and glue to the blue pulp. Blend until well mixed.

**STEP 2** Use a permanent marker to draw the design of your frame on the Plexiglas sheet. Place your mirror on top, facing up. Pick up a small quantity of the colored papier mâché, knead it well so that no air bubbles are in the material and the edges are smooth. Place it on the plastic board, working from the mirror out. Use modeling tools to shape the papier mâché. Cover the entire surface of the plastic board. Be especially careful at the corners of the mirror, so that they won't tear while drying. When you have to combine two colors, work very carefully. Press and soak up the excess water and press with a sponge to prevent the colors from running into each other. Emboss patterns in the surface with modeling tools and other found objects. Reserve a small amount of each color to repair any small breaks that occur during drying.

**STEP 3** Let your mirror dry. This can take from two to ten days. The surface and the outside edges will dry first. It might be necessary to put a weight (stones) on the edges, so your mirror stays flat. If there are breaks, especially where two colors meet, it's better to repair them while your mirror is still a little wet. Put a small amount of glue with a brush unto the edges of the break. Place a small quantity of papier–mâché into the break. Again use a sponge to remove the excess water.

**STEP 4** When the mirror is dry, you can varnish it. (Use water-based acrylic varnish for cool colors and shellac for warmer colors.) Remove the mirror and clean it carefully, then varnish the frame. Next, glue the edges of the papier-mâché where the mirror will be fixed and lay the mirror in place. Take a piece of linen bookbinding tape, cut it to the size of your mirror, and glue it to the back. Loop a piece of twisted paper thread and glue it in the middle of the top edge to make a hanging loop.

*Monika Dimitrakopoulos-Lang*

## TIP

**For a simpler frame, use just in one color and paint it afterwards. Try tempera colors for a watercolor effect. Finish with spray acrylic.**

*This vessel reflects the artist's surroundings—the sun, the moon, the Arizona mountains: it is formed from paper pulp that is cast in halves that are later joined. The vessel is embellished using other natural materials such as feathers, raffia, ribbons, and decorative beads.*

## MATERIALS

- paper for pulp
- unsized paper for surface (soft handmade paper works best)
- white glue
- fabric strips
- course sandpaper
- methylcellulose glue
- marker
- paste wax
- plastic wrap
- sponge
- blender
- acrylic medium, matte or glossy

# STARCATCHER
# CAST-PAPER VESSEL

**STEP 1** Choose a vessel or pot to use as a mold. Tear up pieces of paper to make paper pulp. Put the torn paper through a blender with plenty of water until a soupy slurry of pulp remains. Make enough pulp to cover the basic form. For a filler, add ¼" cup of regular white glue for every gallon of pulp.

**STEP 2** Cover the pot with paste floor wax and mark the half lines with a marker. (You'll only cast half of the pot at a time.) Cover the first half with plastic wrap. This makes it easy to pull off the dry casting. Take slightly drained pulp in handfuls and plop it over the plastic, carefully sponging out the water each time. When the half shape is covered, let it dry completely. Remove the dried half, repeat this step to make another half.

**STEP 3** Fit the two halves together, trimming with scissors to make them fit as tightly as possible. Glue the edges together with white glue and tie a strip of fabric around the shape until dry. Sand the side seams with heavy sandpaper to smooth them out. Glue a strip of thin, soft paper over the entire seam, making sure the bottom is flat and that the pot sits level.

**STEP 4** Tear unsized paper into approximate 2" (5 cm) pieces and glue onto the casting in an overlapping style. Methylcellulose glue is best for this since it's completely invisible when dry. Add decorative elements with other paper shapes, feathers, raffia, ribbon ties, or beads. Cover the entire vessel with a coat of acrylic matte or medium gloss cut by half with water. Use this sturdy, lightweight vessel to display feathers, dried weeds, or whatever strikes your fancy.

*Pat Baldwin*

## MATERIALS

- decorated handmade paper from cotton, abaca, kozo, iris, and cornhusk
- large mold and deckle

*Though shown here as a runner, this intricate and beautiful piece may also be framed and hung. The artist uses pieces of previously formed handmade papers of various fiber types. The papers are decorated using encaustic painting, and printmaking techniques such as etching, block printing, and linoleum printing. The artist combines pure pigments with waxes: The mixture is heated and then painted onto the surface of the paper.*

Helene Zucco

# PAINTED RUNNER

**STEP 1** Make and/or decorate various styles of handmade papers.

**STEP 2** Cut the finished papers into mosaic like pieces. Fit the pieces together first to work out your design. Arrange the papers facedown onto the screen of a large mold and deckle, and dampen them. Add beads, bamboo, and other printed materials into the mosaic to add texture and surface interest.

**STEP 3** Add a second layer of cotton pulp. Press it lightly to ease the air out, but don't sponge it down.

**STEP 4** Allow the piece to dry, and remove from the mold and deckle. Add fringe. The artist uses shifu, a Japanese technique of taking mulberry paper and twisting it in your fingers to make a thread, somewhat like making drop-spindle wool.

*Make fanciful floral shades for a strand of lights by using colorful papers and papier-mâché paste. The paste makes the shapes quite sturdy and long-lasting. The trick is using an ice-cube tray to create the "cup" of the flower. With that as the base, it is easy to build the additional layers. Perfect for a patio or deck, these paper light strands will add a festive feeling to any gathering.*

**MATERIALS**

- white, yellow, orange, and aqua handmade papers
- papier-mâché art paste
- scissors
- craft knife
- plastic ice-cube tray
- vegetable oil
- metal ruler
- round shapes to trace

# LIGHT STRAND SHADES

**STEP 1** Mix the papier-mâché paste according to package directions in an air-tight container. Wipe the inside of the ice-cube tray lightly with vegetable oil.

**STEP 2** Tear the rice paper into 1" x 2" (3 cm x 5 cm) pieces. Dip the pieces into the paste, and squeeze off any excess. Line the inside of each ice-cube compartment with a layer of white paper and let dry. Repeat with another layer of white paper. When the paper has dried completely, remove the paper cups from the tray.

**STEP 3** Cut a doughnut-shaped piece of yellow paper about 5" (13 cm) in diameter, with a 1" (3 cm) hole in the center. Make a cut through each doughnut, dip into the paste, and place on each paper cup, like a skirt. Overlap the cut sides to fit the skirt to the cup. Let dry on a flat, smooth surface (like a Formica counter) so the paper won't stick.

**STEP 4** When all the skirts are dry, cut six petal shapes for each cup out of the orange paper. Using the paste as before, glue six petals around each skirted cup and let dry. Finally, cut four or five 2" (5 cm) circles for each cup out of the aqua paper and glue them around the cup. Let dry.

**STEP 5** Cut a small X with a craft knife in the top of each paper cup to insert the mini tree lights.

*Janet Pensiero*

## MATERIALS

*for the rainbow mobile:*

- cooking screen (like those used to trap splattering oil)
- window screening cut into various-sized circles
- blender or Hollander beater
- 2 vats or tubs
- 2 pieces of wood for pressing (4" [10 cm] longer than diameter of the screen) pieces of fabric (as long as the wood each way)
- scissors
- 24 (720 g) ounces of paper in each of 6 rainbow colors (4 ounces [120 g] of each color)
- string
- embroidery hoop

## MATERIALS

*for the paper blocks*

- strong cardboard boxes in different sizes and shapes
- newspaper

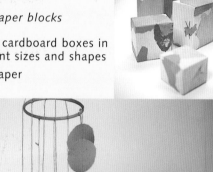

*Monika Dimitrakopoulis-Lang*

- tape
- beautiful, strong paper
- glue
- water-based acrylic sealer
- brush

*The artist was influenced by the opinions of the Waldorf school and anthroposophy\* that the usual wooden bricks are too small for small children, so she has designed large, soft, light-weight paper bricks of all sizes, even two and three feet high, that can be stacked and played with. As an artist and teacher, she has used papermaking as an activity to teach children about color and recycling. For the mobile, the children use simple wire screen circles without a deckle to draw the pulp.*

*\*Anthroposophy is a spiritual and mystical philosophy based on the teachings of Rudolph Steiner.*

# RAINBOW MOBILE & BUILDING BLOCKS

### Paper Blocks
**STEP 1** Fill the boxes with torn and wadded up newspaper so that they get more durable and resistant to pressure. Fill all the corners, but do not to overstuff.

**STEP 2** Tape the boxes closed using paper tape. Reinforce the corners with extra tape.

**STEP 3** Tear the paper for the outside into irregular pieces. Apply glue with a brush both to the box and the back of the paper. Place the paper on the boxes, and smooth it down securely. Cover it entirely with one to two layers of torn decorative paper. Glue down any loose paper edges. Let dry.

**STEP 4** Varnish the paper bricks with two coats of water-based acrylic sealer.

### Rainbow mobile
**STEP 1** Tear the paper into 1/2" (1 cm) pieces and boil it in water for thirty minutes (boil each color separately). Leave it overnight. Blend it or use a beater to create a pulp.

**STEP 2** Put water in two vats and add one color of pulp. Form one round sheet by dipping the mold into the vat and catching the fibers. Couch it on a piece of felt. Put the thread in the shape of a spiral on the first sheet. Form another sheet with the second color and couch it onto the first sheet. Press both well before removing the mold, to bind the fibers. Continue the process using the smaller molds until you have three pieces. If there is enough pulp left, make some extra sheets for repairing, and so on. Empty your vats and continue repeating this step with the other colors.

**STEP 3** Press the paper. Sandwich the felted papers between newspaper and pressing boards and weight it. Let dry.

**STEP 4** Carefully remove the finished paper and construct your mobile. Sandwich same-sized paper around pieces of string and tie them around the hoop. Suspend the hoop from a hook.

*The colorful collage on this wall light is not really quilted in the true sense of the word; it is made by piecing papers together on a sewing machine using zigzag and other decorative types of stitching. The final papers are mounted on screening over a wooden frame. The light is designed to hang on a wall with the wires traveling through a lamp pipe that extends from the bottom.*

## MATERIALS

- assortment of handmade and commercial papers
- sewing machine
- thread in various colors
- crochet cotton
- two 22" (56 cm) pine 1' x 4' (.3 m x 1.2 m)
- two 20 1/2" (52 cm) pine 1' x 4' (.3 m x 1.2 m)
- hammer and nails
- drill
- hardware cloth
- yellow or gold-toned tissue paper
- red spray paint
- lamp holders (Leviton #9882 used here)

# QUILTED WALL LIGHT

**STEP 1** Form a square wood frame from two 22" (56 cm) pine 1' x 4' (.3 m x 1.2 m) and two 20 1/2" (52 cm) pine 1' x 4' (.3 m x 1.2 m), nailing the corners together. Drill five 1" (3 cm) diameter holes in the top piece (for heat release) and one 3/8" (1 cm) diameter hole in the bottom. Paint the frame as desired. Mount and wire four lamp holders equidistant around the inside of the frame with the wire ending at the hole at bottom. Thread a nut onto the wire inside of the frame, then thread the wire through the bottom hole and through the pipe. Insert 28" (71 cm) length of lamp pipe in hole and secure with another nut. Wire a switch and plug at end of the wire. Wrap the pipe with fiber, if desired.

**STEP 2** Cut hardware cloth to fit the square. Spray-paint the hardware cloth to protect the paper from the metal. Cover with thin tissue, tucking under at edges. (The artist uses dip-dyed model airplane tissue but says you can substitute gift tissue.) Nail the hardware cloth to the frame.

**STEP 3** Machine stitch together strips of handmade and commercial papers of varying colors. Use zigzag and other decorative stitching and various colors of thread. Cut and piece until a pleasing composition of approximately 22" (56 cm) square is achieved. Cut the square into quarters. Cut four shapes approximately 11" (28 cm) square out of wire window screening. Bind each edge with a 1" (3 cm) strip of paper, halved and sewn on like bias tape. Stitch the collages onto the window screening by machine or by hand.

**STEP 4** Hand stitch each square to the hardware cloth using crochet cotton or a similar weight thread. Leave gaps where the light will appear brighter. Screw 25-watt tubular bulbs into the fixtures. Insert eyes in frame and hang from picture wire.

*Jennifer Morrow Wilson*

- 2 nuts
- 28" (71 cm) length of lamp pipe
- light switch and wall plug
- hardware cloth
- 24-watt tubular bulbs
- picture-hanging wire
- eye hooks

## MATERIALS

- shiny card stock

- tissue or crepe paper that will bleed

- spray bottle of water

- hole punch

- grommet tool and grommets or double-sided tape

- scissors

- tiny nails

- sticks (use small dowels, balsa wood, pencils, or twigs)

*These dazzling pinwheels will really get noticed. Perfect for birthdays or summer parties, they are so quick and simple to make that you won't mind if everyone takes them home as favors—and they'll want to. Any that are left can be disassembled and stored flat until the next party. Small ones make cute place cards. Medium ones enliven potted plants, or, if you haven't any flowers, stick them in a bowl of greens as a colorful kinetic centerpiece. Of course, they are wonderful lining the driveway or fluttering in the garden. The pinwheels featured are made from squares of card-stock paper. This is perfect for showing off your latest decorated paper technique, but old posters and other papers work well too. Keep in mind that both sides of the paper will show.*

# PAPER PINWHEELS

**STEP 1** Cut shiny card stock into squares of any size. To decorate the card stock, use colorful papers that will bleed when wet, such as tissue papers, crepe papers, or construction paper. Tear the colored paper into pieces and place them on the background paper. Overlap a few. Spritz or sprinkle the papers with water. Be sure the colors you choose are compatible because they will run and mingle, creating other colors. Let the card stock dry. Or get two decorated pieces at once by placing another piece of card stock over the dye papers, press down to make contact and let the whole "sandwich" dry. Be sure to decorate the backside of the card stock for pinwheels.

**STEP 2** From each corner of the square, make a diagonal cut toward the center, to within 1" (3 cm) of the center. Bend every other point to the center and punch holes through all layers of paper to join them. For permanent use, install a grommet through the five holes. Nail, through the holes, to a stick. For non-permanent use, secure the points with double-sided tape, punch a hole through all and attach to a stick. When the party is over, remove the tape and store flat.

Nancy Welch

*Make a quick column lamp that is lit on the inside by a hanging strand of tree lights. You can purchase paper with wire already embedded or make your own. To make your own, bend your wire into the desired shape, then measure and wrap a sheet of paper around the form. Coat the entire structure with acrylic medium to bind the paper and wire together. The embedded wire makes the lamp sturdy and adds an interesting shadow to the lamp when lit. You can experiment using different colors of paper, or make lamps like this in any size. Use them outdoors with candles in warmer weather.*

## MATERIALS

- 21" x 27" (53 cm x 68.5 cm) sheet chicken wire laminated with paper
- dark green charcoal paper
- light green charcoal paper
- 14-gauge armature wire
- scissors
- ruler
- wire cutter
- hot glue gun
- white glue
- work gloves

# LIGHTED SCULPTURE

**STEP 1** Wearing gloves to protect your hands, fold over the two long edges of the wire paper twice to a width of 1" (3 cm) so that the edge of the chicken wire is completely enclosed. Fold over one shorter edge the same way.

**STEP 2** Cut a piece of dark green paper 4" (10 cm) wide and equal to the length of the shorter edge of the paper. Fold the paper in half lengthwise, and glue around the edge. Cut four 3" x 7" (8 cm x 18 cm) rectangles from light green paper. Glue these at equally spaced intervals along the length of the dark green strip, folding them in half and wrapping them around the edge as you did with the dark green.

**STEP 3** Roll the entire sheet into a column, with the green edge in front. Hot glue the green edge to secure. Bend a piece of wire into an oval spiral, approximately 1" x 2" (3 cm x 5 cm), leaving a 1/2" (1 cm) perpendicular piece at the end. Push this piece into the bottom light green rectangle paper, fold down the wire inside, and hot glue the inside wire to secure. Repeat to decorate the next three green squares. For the top square, don't trim the perpendicular wire; instead, allow for an extended piece of wire that will span the inside of the column and through to the back. Use hot glue to secure on the outside back of the column. Lay a folded string of fifty tree lights over this cross wire to illuminate your lamp.

*Janet Pensiero*

- 20 vintage postcards,
  3 ¹/2 " x 5 ¹/2 " (9 cm x 14 cm)
  horizontal format

- cylindrical electric light

*Use postcards to create a stylish stacked light fixture. Because each floor of cards is staggered, the sculpture allows the light to shine out through various open spaces in the sculpture. The appearance is much like a house of cards; the structure is carefully built by hinging the slits in the cards together.*

# POSTCARD LIGHT

**STEP 1** For the bottom row, cut two slits in five cards, ⁵/8 " (1.5 cm) in from each edge, 1 ⁷/8 "(4.75 cm) high. Make the slit on the left side extend from the bottom edge up, and the slit on the right side from the top edge down. Use the slits to create an interlocking circle of five postcards. (See pattern diagram on page 124.)

**STEP 2** For the next three rows, cut slits as above in all the remaining cards, plus two more slits, to allow the second and third rows of cards to sit on each other and create the cylindrical shape of the lamp. These additional two slits should be at the bottom edge of the card, and be 1 ¹/2 " (4 cm) in from each side and 1 ¹/8 " (3 cm) high. To assemble the upper rows, connect five cards as before, and then place that construction on the previous row, aligned so that the inner two slits straddle the intersection of the two interlocked cards on the row below. Make the lamp taller by adding additional rows.

**STEP 3** Place the column of interlocked cards over an electric light fixture.

*Janet Pensiero*

*Add exotic glamour to a bathroom cabinet by covering it with Chinese joss papers. Traditionally, joss papers are small rectangular pieces of tissue with a center area of metallic leaf. They are available in Chinese markets and are burned on holidays to commemorate and send good wishes to the departed.*

**MATERIALS**

- wooden cabinet
- gold and/or silver joss paper
- scissors
- fine sandpaper
- acrylic matte medium
- polyurethane
- brushes
- masking tape
- general craft supplies

# JOSS-PAPER BATH CABINET

**STEP 1** Cut around the gold squares of the joss paper and set aside. You'll need about seventy squares to cover the outside of a small cabinet. Prepare the cabinet by lightly sanding the wood and wiping it clean with a damp sponge. Tape paper onto the mirror to protect it from glue and varnish.

**STEP 2** Brush acrylic matte medium onto the back of one of the paper squares and apply to the cabinet. Press down and smooth out the paper to eliminate any air bubbles. Overlap the papers slightly so there are no gaps showing. Be careful not to touch the surface of the joss paper with sticky fingers as the surface is quite fragile and the leaf could come off. Keep a damp cloth nearby to wipe your fingers and catch any spills. Repeat this process until the entire cabinet is covered. Trim the joss paper into smaller pieces to fit specific areas of the cabinet. Allow paper to completely dry.

**STEP 3** Coat the cabinet with three layers of polyurethane, drying thoroughly between coats, to protect the delicate surface from wear and tear. Once dry, remove the paper from the mirror.

## TIP

To vary your design, cover the inside of the cabinet with a contrasting paper or paint. Or, combine both gold and silver papers to create a mosaic pattern. You can also antique the paper after application by applying a thin wash of burnt umber oil paint with a rag. And finally, consider replacing the mirror with chicken wire or glass to create a curio display cabinet.

*Paula Grasdal*

## MATERIALS

- wooden vase
- ivory doilies
- butterfly decoupage scraps
- garden decoupage scraps
- light green acrylic paint
- white acrylic paint
- satin decoupage finish
- fine-tip brown permanent marker
- 1" (3 cm) wide brush
- decoupage scissors
- #220 sandpaper
- craft knife

*One of the most delightful aspects of decoupage is that it can be used to decorate almost any surface. It's a perfect craft for beginners or for creative people who want to make highly personalized furnishings and gifts. And while decoupage doesn't require high-level artistic experience, the results can be spectacular.*

Connie Sheerin

# DECOUPAGED VASE

**STEP 1** Fill any holes or imperfections with wood putty and allow to dry. Sand the vase, removing any rough spots. Paint two coats of base color onto the vase. Allow to dry. Take a damp brush and dip into white paint to streak the base color for a chalky effect.

**STEP 2** Using decoupage scissors, cut out all of your butterfly and garden designs, removing all of the white background. Cut several parts out of the doily to use as trim on base of vase.

**STEP 3** Randomly place round doilies onto vase, using the satin coat decoupage finish that will also act as your glue. Paint a coat onto the doily as well as on the wood. Place the doily on the vase, smoothing out all wrinkles with a damp paper towel. Next, glue on all the garden objects, smoothing out all wrinkles with a damp paper towel. Repeat to add butterflies. If you are having trouble getting out the air bubbles, make a small slit with a craft knife and then smooth the area flat with a wet paper towel. Allow the prints to dry thoroughly.

**STEP 4** Use a permanent marker to draw antennae onto the butterflies. With a brush, paint on several coats of satin varnish, changing the direction of your brush strokes between each layer. Dry thoroughly between coats.

*Backgrounds stamps are becoming increasingly popular and work well to create an all-over pattern on simple paper accessories like this switchplate and frame. The stamped pattern is highlighted with embossing powder to add texture and heighten the color. The wonderful stamps used here are designed by the artist. (See the Resources list for details.)*

## MATERIALS

*For the switchplate:*

- light switch
- 4" x 2" (10 cm x 5 cm) sturdy illustration board
- 6"x 4" (15 cm x 10 cm) black sheet of paper
- 'winged post collage' rubber stamp
- white pigment stamp pad
- white (or glow-in-the-dark) embossing powder
- heat tool
- ruler
- glue
- craft knife

# PAPER SWITCHPLATE &
# PAPER FRAME

**SWITCHPLATE**

**STEP 1** Measure the centerlines from top to bottom and side to side on the piece of illustration board. From the two shorter sides (top and bottom of plate), measure 1 3/4" (4.5 cm) from each side and mark the lines with a pencil. From the two longer sides, measure 1 3/16" (1.5 cm) from each side and mark these two lines with pencil.

**STEP 2** Cut the inner 3/8" x 15/16" (1 cm x 1 cm) rectangle (for the light switch) with a craft knife. For the screw holes, use a mini-hole punch and punch each hole on the centerline, one inch from each short side (top and bottom of the plate).

**STEP 3** Stamp the 'winged post collage' repeatedly on the black sheet of paper in white ink. Immediately sprinkle white embossing powder all over the stamped image and emboss with a heat tool.

Once the paper is cool, turn it over (the wrong side facing you) and coat with glue. Center the switchplate board on the paper. Using a craft knife, cut an X in the light switch area and fold each side toward the wrong side of the plate. Adhere firmly. Glue the sides of the stamped paper back to the wrong side of the plate. Repunch the screw holes with the hole punch. Let the plate dry and then screw in place.

**FRAME**

**STEP 1** Take one of the larger identical boards and cut a 3 1/2" x 5" (9 cm x 13 cm) window out, leaving a 1" (3 cm) border on all sides. Save the cut out window piece; it will become your stand.

**STEP 2** Stamp the 'on the metro wall' stamp all over the frame. Immediately sprinkle the silver embossing powder and emboss the stamped images.

**STEP 3** Insert and tape in your favorite photo. Hot glue the two larger boards together exactly. Cut the saved window piece as shown in pattern diagram on page 124. Position this piece at the center bottom and hot glue in place.

*Dawn Houser*

*For the frame:*

- two 5 1/2" x 7" (14 cm x 18 cm) pieces of black illustration board
- 'on the metro wall' rubber stamp
- silver pigment inkpad
- silver embossing powder
- craft knife
- heat tool
- hot glue gun
- ruler

## MATERIALS

- Japanese papers
- 2" (5 cm) bristle brush
- small bowl of water
- acrylic paints
- stiff brush
- an object to cover

*The candlesticks here are cast iron, covered with pale green Japanese mulberry paper and black and copper paint. Japanese papers work well for a project like this because the fibers are long, strong, and durable. Any wood, plastic, or metal item can be covered with paper and accented with paint to create an entirely new look. If wood is unfinished or if the metal might rust, seal the item with acrylic paint before you begin. This technique allows you to really transform any object—as long as it has a wonderful shape or silhouette.*

# PAPERED IRON CANDLESTICKS

**STEP 1** If necessary, coat your object entirely with acrylic paint. Tear the paper to be used into small pieces. Quickly pull a piece through the water. Hold it with both hands to spread it; it will get translucent. Lay the wet sheet on the object to be covered and brush out any air bubbles. Use the brush in a pouncing motion to mat down the fibers and ease the paper into any grooves. Tear another small sheet of paper and repeat, overlapping the first piece. (Because wet paper sticks to itself, no glue is needed in this process.) Continue laying wet sheets down until the object is entirely covered (back and front). Don't worry about where you are putting the torn edges of the papers, they won't show when the piece is dry; in fact they add to the textural interest.

**STEP 2** Allow the piece to dry. When the paper dries, it will shrink tightly around the object, revealing the sculptural details. After the paper dries, you can see any places you missed.
To cover these areas, wet some more bits of paper and add them. You can use a wet brush, as needed.

**STEP 3** When paper is completely dry, highlight the lines and textures by using the dry-brush technique. Squeeze out a little acrylic paint onto a palette or board. Using a stiff brush, spread the paint out and get a little of it on the brush. Using a very light touch, gently drag the brush over the paper surface to pick up the high points of the surface. In this case, I used a bit of black first and then copper acrylic paint to finish.

*Carol Cole*

*Make a quick and charming votive shade using an attractive rubber stamp and adding glitter glue for sparkle. The basic shape is made from laminated vellum and secured with curled strands of silver wire. You can use this basic technique to make shades of any size.*

## MATERIALS

- 8 ½" x 11" (22 cm x 28 cm) sheet of vellum
- 'zebra butterfly' rubber stamp
- black inkpad
- colored glitter glue
- hole punch
- 28-gauge wire
- votive candle

# STAMPED VOTIVE SHADE

**STEP 1** Stamp the butterfly in all directions all over the vellum. Let dry.

**STEP 2** Apply several glitter glue colors to the wings of each butterfly. Let dry.

**STEP 3** Laminate the vellum. Lay the laminated piece over newspaper and make pinpricks in a looping pattern around the surface of the shade.

**STEP 4** Punch holes on the short length of each side of the laminated vellum, matching the holes up carefully.

**STEP 5** Form the vellum into a lantern shape and twist lengths of wire through each pair of holes and into decorative curls to secure the edges.

*Dawn Houser*

## MATERIALS

- 14" x 2 1/2" (36 cm x 6 cm) colored art paper (or any paper of a 65-pound cover weight)

- 3" x 8" (8 cm x 20 cm) backing paper

- 7" x 2 1/2" (18 cm x 6 cm) decorative paper such as marbled paper (to be glued to top of cover paper)

- ruled or unlined paper

- 8" x 2 1/2" (20 cm x 6 cm) one sheet minimum

- 8 1/2" x 2 1/2" (22 cm x 6 cm) one sheet minimum

- 9" x 2 1/2" (23 cm x 6 cm) one sheet minimum

- 20" (51 cm) ribbon or thin cording

- 20" (51 cm) pearl cotton or thread

- 2" x 2" (5 cm x 5 cm) wide ribbon or decorative paper

- alphabet letter stamps and ink pad, or adhesive lettering

- white glue or glue stick

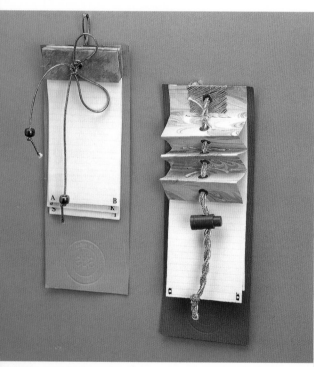

*Susan Jaworski-Stranc*

- cutting board or 8" x 10" (20 cm x 25 cm) foam core

- straightedge

- mat knife

- sewing needle

- bone folder

- hole punch

*Keep frequently called numbers hanging right near the phone in a beautiful handmade paper booklet. You will use a simple pamphlet stitch to attach the booklet pages to an accordion-pleated cover. A decorative cord allows you to loosen or gather the pages together and also provides a hanging loop at the back.*

## ROMAN SHADE PHONE BOOK

**STEP 1** Take the color art paper, 14" x 2 1/2" (36 cm x 6 cm) and fold in half. If you are planning to cover the top of colored art paper with the 7" x 2 1/2" (18 cm x 6 cm) decorative paper, do so next; then continue. Using a bone folder, score six lines at 1-inch (3 cm) intervals. Accordion-pleat the paper. With paper still folded into pleats, take a pencil and mark the center on the face of the top pleat. Paper-punch this mark through all layers. If paper is too thick, take a sewing needle and pierce through all layers at the center mark. Then open the paper slightly, and paper-punch two layers (or one fold) at a time.

**STEP 2** It is important to correctly orient the folded paper for proper accordion-folding sequence of "peaks" (up) and "valleys" (down). The top edge of paper project is the open end of folded paper and it begins with the "peak" and the next fold, being the first true scored fold is the "valley." All book pages are stitched on the backside of "valley" folds. Take the sewing needle and pierce three holes in each of the three "valley" folds, marked at 1/2", 1 1/2", and 2" (1 cm, 3.5 cm, and 5 cm).

**STEP 3** Fold all book pages in half. Place the open fold of the longest sheet (9" [23 cm]) against the bottom of the first "valley" fold. Use paper clips or binder clips to keep the page in position. With a sewing needle, re-pierce through the holes. Thread the needle and sew this page to the cover using a pamphlet stitch. Repeat to attach the 8 1/2" (22 cm) page sewn along the middle "valley" fold and the 8" (20 cm) page along the third "valley."

**STEP 4** Print, stamp, or adhere letters to the bottom edge of each page. The last page sewn begins the alphabet listings of A and B. You can group the letters in any fashion. Just remember you have twelve pages to organize twenty-six letters.

**STEP 5** Glue the backside of the first pleat to the backing paper. Re-punch the paper hole. Fold the wide ribbon in half and glue it over the top edge. Paper-punch hole again. Fold ribbons or cording in half and make a knotted loop approximately 1 inch (3 cm) from fold. Press the accordion-folded cover together. Thread the ends of ribbon/cord through the backside of cover, passing through all holes to the front. Now, elongate the cover by gently pulling open the folds. There should be plenty of ribbon/cording extending past the last hole. Decorate the ends with beads if you wish. To gather up the cover and pages, just pull on the ribbon while compressing the folds. Tie with a bow to secure. Hang near the phone using the loop at the top.

# CONTRIBUTING ARTISTS

**Pat Baldwin**
Waterleaf Mill & Bindery
Pequeño Press
P.O. Box 1711
Bisbee, AZ 85603
Tel: (520) 432-5924

**Carol Cole**
346 Llandrillo Road
Bala Cynwyd, PA 19004
Tel: (610) 664-2825
http:///www.carolcole.com

**Monika Dimitrakopoulos-Lang**
Sklipi 62, GR-84100 Ermoupolis
Syros, Kyklades, Greece
Tel/Fax: 0030/281/84-487
http://www.papersun.de.vu

**Paula Grasdal**
437 Trapelo Road
Belmont, MA 02478
Tel: (617) 489-4717

**Linda Louise Horn**
618 Leverington Avenue
Philadelphia, PA 19128
Tel: (215) 509-7433

**Dawn Houser**
418 Laramie Drive
San Antonio, TX 78209
Tel: (210) 930-0373
www.dawnhouser.com

**Elizabeth Kosterich**
Paper and Clay Studios, LLC
4725 Dorsey Hall Drive, Suite A, PMB 503
Ellicott City, MD  21042
Tel: (410) 992-1431

**Fran Lacy**
Lacy Design
8569 N. 275 W.
Delphi, IN 46923
Tel: (219) 686-2922

**Livia McRee**
103 Charles Street, #42W
New York, NY 10014
Tel: (646) 336-1816
www.liviamcree.cm

**Janet Pensiero**
263 Dupont Street
Philadelphia, PA 19128
Tel: (215) 487-2553

**Winnie Radolan**
Winnie's Paperworks
5064 McKean Avenue
Philadelphia, PA 19144
Tel: (215) 844-6388

**Connie Sheerin**
Crafts ala Cart
P.O. Box 246
Lansdowne, PA 19050
Tel: (973) 657-1612

**Susan Jaworski-Stranc**
Apple Cider Press & Prints
Newbury, MA 01951
Tel: (978) 465-9896

**Kathleen Trenchard**
Cut-It-Out®
P.O. Box 120232
San Antonio, TX 78212
www.cut-it-out.org

**Nancy Welch**
801 La Honda Road
Woodside, CA 94062

**Jennifer Morrow Wilson**
Box 311A Eggemoggin Road
Little Deer Isle, ME 04650
Tel: (207) 348-6871

**Helene Zucco**
186 Lake Road
Fleetwood, PA 19522
Tel: (610) 944-9061
www.napconn.org

# RESOURCES LIST

**Artifacts Inc.**
P.O. Box 3399
Palestine, TX 75801
Tel: (903) 729-4178
http://www.artifactsinc.com/
Victorian decoupage scraps

**Create an Impression**
56 E. Lancaster Avenue
Ardmore, PA 19003
Tel: (610) 645-6500
handmade papers, stamps, arts and crafts supplies

**Dieu Donné Papermill, Inc.**
433 Broome Street
New York, NY 10013
Tel: (877) 337-2737 or
(212) 226-0573
http://www.colophon.com/dieudonne/
custom papers, papermaking supplies, workshops

**Fascinating Folds**
P.O. Box 10070
Glendale, AZ 85318
Tel: (800) 968-2418
http://www.fascinating-folds.com
supplies for paper arts

**Inkadinkado**
61 Holton Street
Woburn, MA 01801
Tel: (800) 888-4652
http://www.inkadinkado.com
Daydreams Collection by Dawn Houser and
other rubber stamps

**Lee Scott McDonald, Inc.**
P.O. Box 264
Charlestown, MA 02129
Tel: (617) 242-2505 or toll free: (888) 627-2737
papermaking supplies

**Loose Ends**
P.O. Box 20310
Salem, OR 97307
Tel: (503) 390-7457
http://www.looseends.com
papers, packaging, natural paraphernalia

**Magnolia Editions**
2527 Magnolia Street
Oakland, CA
Tel: (510) 839-5268
http://www.artfolio.com/magnolia/frame.htm
papermaking supplies and workshops

**Paper Source**
232 West Chicago Avenue
Chicago, IL 60610
Tel: (312) 337-0798
(stores also in Evanston, Kansas City, Philadelphia,
and Cambridge)
handmade papers and stamps

**Kate's Paperie**
561 Broadway
New York, NY 10012
Tel: (888) 941-9169
http://www.katespaperie.com/
handmade papers and stationery

**The Paper Crane**
280 Cabot Street
Beverly, MA 01915
Tel: (978) 927-3131

**Rugg Road**
105 Charles Street
Boston, MA 02114
Tel: (617) 742-0002
handmade papers and stationery

**Scratch**
100 Levering Street
Manayunk, PA 19127
Tel: (215) 508-9797
papers and art supplies

**Twinrocker**
P.O. Box 413
Brookston, IN 47923
Tel: (800) 757-8946
http://dcwi.com/~twinrock/Welcome.html
handmade papers and stationery

**Yasutomo**
490 Eccles Avenue
South San Francisco, CA 94080-1901
Tel: (650) 737-8888
http://www.yasutomo.com
wholesaler of rayon papers and other art supplies

**Xyron Inc.**
15820 North 84th Street
Scottsdale, AZ 85260
Tel: (800) 793-3523
http://www.xyron.com/
laminating machines

PERIODICALS
**Hand Papermaking**
P.O. Box 77027
Washington, DC 20013-7027
Tel: (800) 821-6604
http://www.bookarts.com/handpapermaking/

ORGANIZATIONS
**Friends of Dard Hunter**
P.O. Box 773
Lake Oswego, OR 97034
http://www.slis.ua.edu/ba/dardo.html

**IAPMA** (International Association of Hand Papermakers and
Paper Artists)
Fredensgade 4
Stryno, Ryudkobing
DK-5900 Denmark
IAPMA Secretary: Eva Maria Juras
http://www.design.dk/org/iapma/

# P A T T E R N S  *by Natalie Wenholtz*

## Photocopy at 100%

Postcard Light Diagram

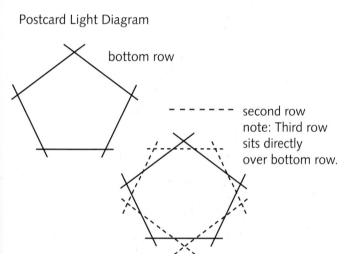

bottom row

second row
note: Third row
sits directly
over bottom row.

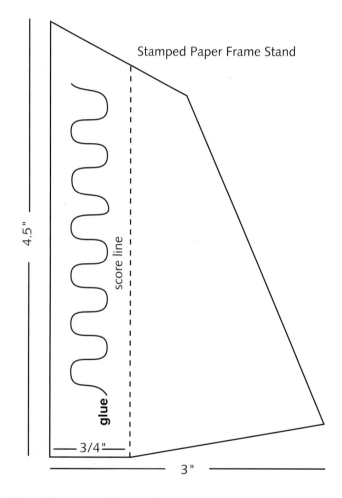

Stamped Paper Frame Stand

4.5"

score line

glue

3/4"

3"

Photocopy at 200%

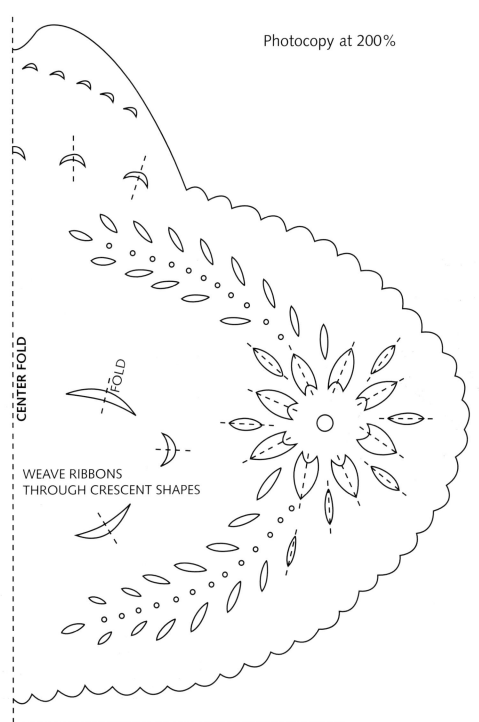

CENTER FOLD

FOLD

WEAVE RIBBONS
THROUGH CRESCENT SHAPES

MEXICAN SOMBRERO PLACE MAT CUTTING DIAGRAM

PBA-01 Paper Strip Lipstick Cabinet
Photocopy at 200%

PB-05
Pin-pricked Vellum Night-light Shade Bee

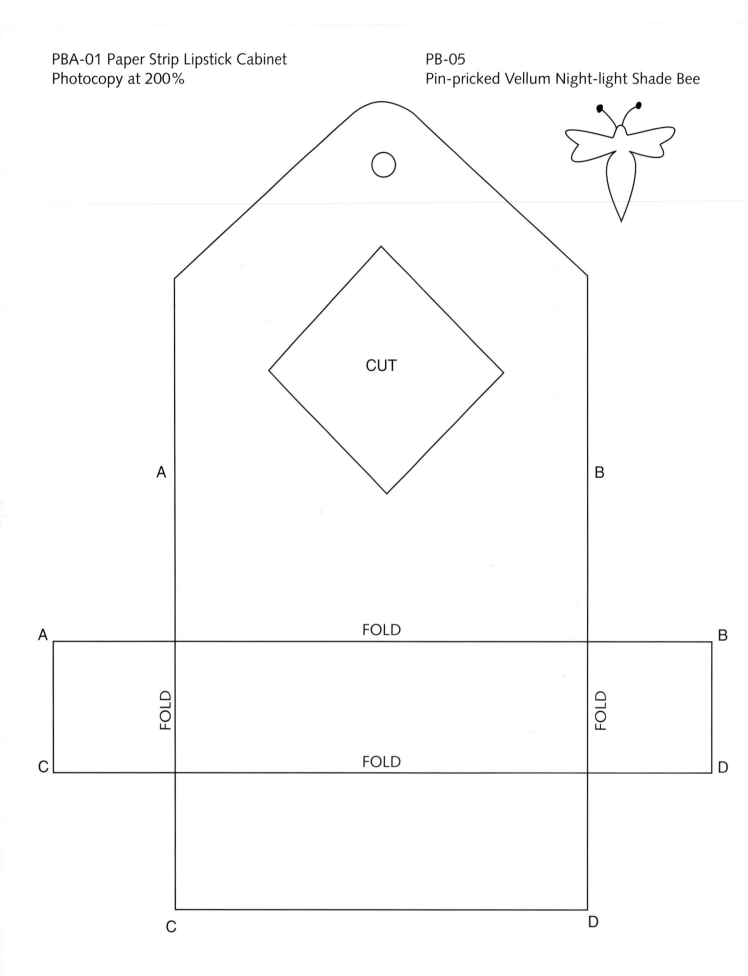

CUT

A

B

A

FOLD

B

FOLD

FOLD

FOLD

FOLD

C

FOLD

D

C

D

# ACKNOWLEDGMENTS

I want to thank several people whose important contributions made this book possible. First, I'd like to thank Livia McRee, who helped me construct several of the projects that I designed for this book. She is a wonderful colleague and friend, and an extremely talented designer in her own right. I thank her for her excellent work and valuable feedback. I'm also very grateful to my wise and delightful editor, Shawna Mullen, and to the team at Rockport who have assisted in this project. They have made the task of pulling all this together a joy. Thank you all.

I also thank all the artists who contributed their works for the gallery section of this book. It has been a pleasure to work with and learn from all of you. And thanks to Leigh and Layne Lyons, owners of Helene Zucco's piece, for lending your artwork for photography. Thanks also to Dawn Houser for providing her artwork for the paper frame projects and to Kathleen Trenchard, whose paper cut placemat was featured in the kitchen chapter.

Sincere appreciation also goes to Sandi, Art, Jason, and all the folks at Loose Ends for their enthusiasm for paper arts. They supplied me with samples of and information about many of the beautiful papers used in this book. I'd also like to thank Brian Welton, and everyone at Kate's Paperie, for their assistance and for providing samples. Thanks also to Yuki for the inspiration for the window streamers. Thanks to Connie Sheerin and Sandra Salamony for your humor and friendship, always, but particularly during our simultaneous projects. And thanks to all of my former colleagues at Craftopia.com for your kindness and encouragement.

Lastly, I'd like to thank my mom and family for always appreciating my creative interests, and my husband Chris, who is infinitely patient, kind, and insightful, and always able to keep me laughing—even when the house is strewn with half-finished projects (which seems to be all the time).

## ABOUT THE AUTHOR

**Mary Ann Hall** *is a writer and editor with an enduring interest in arts, crafts, and design. She is currently an acquisitions editor for Rockport Publishers. Prior to this, she was the founding editor and director of content of* **Craftopia.com** *and she was the editor-in-chief of* **Handcraft Illustrated***, a leading craft and home-decorating magazine. She has contributed to several books, most recently as the curator of over eighty projects featured in* **The Crafter's Project Book** *(Rockport Publishers, 2000) and as a project designer and writer for Country Living's Handmade Frames (Hearst Communications, 1999). As a longtime artist and crafter, she has studied and worked in several areas, including jewelry and metalworking, painting, polymer-clay sculpture, glassblowing, and furniture making. She currently resides in Lionville, Pennsylvania with her husband Chris and their much-loved cat.*